SEARCHING FOR YOUR ANCESTORS

SEARCHING
FOR YOUR ANCESTORS

The How and Why of Genealogy

BY

GILBERT H. DOANE, F.A.S.G.

*"Think not that the nobilitie of your
Ancestors doth free you to doe all that
you list, contrarywise, it bindeth you
more to followe vertue."*

PIERRE ERONDELL

UNIVERSITY OF MINNESOTA PRESS · Minneapolis

Nov. 5, 1974
74-162861

Library of Congress Catalog Card Number: 60-12200
ISBN 0-8166-0213-1

THIS BOOK *is dedicated to those of my*
ancestors who were proficient in reading
pedigrees, and especially to my
great-great-grandmother

SARAH SOULE MERRILL SMITH

1782–1867

at whose stern likeness, rising from undulating
billows of black satin and capped with linen
and lace, I gaze with awe and reluctant admira-
tion when I turn to it in the family album; and
to my wife

SUSAN HOWLAND SHERMAN DOANE

who, for fifty years, has indulged me as I have
searched for my ancestors and hers even when
we were on our honeymoon, much of which was
spent copying gravestone inscriptions in north-
ern Vermont

Preface

This book is intended to be an introduction to the method of searching for elusive and forgotten ancestors. It has been written primarily for the individual who has always thought that he would look up the family tree, but has never got around to it. The average person never does get around to it, mainly because he does not know how to start, and feels a bit sheepish, perhaps, about asking a librarian for directions. This book is designed also for the librarian of the public library in order that he may have something to put into the hands of patrons who have decided to look up their ancestors and come to him for advice.

A word of warning to prospective searchers for ancestors: do your own digging, at least at the beginning or until you have found out enough about your family to have definite problems which you want to solve. When you have done as much as you think you can or seem to have struck a ledge of rock in your digging, then consult with or take your problem to a genealogist of good repute. But beware of circular letters which come to you unsolicited through the mails offering to supply a complete history of your family on receipt of your check. Do not waste your money on widely advertised genealogical services which appear to promise you your lineage back to the emigrant ancestor. If you fall for their subtle appeal to pride, you are likely to receive a pamphlet containing a few paragraphs on the origin of your surname, a few statements about the most prominent people of that name (which appeals, of course, to your vanity by implying that you are definitely connected with them), and a record, which may or may not be authentic, of the first few generations of the family in America. Proof of your own connection with the emigrants probably will not be given, and in the end you will in all likelihood find yourself with your same old problem and minus the money you have remitted.

There are reputable and reliable genealogists, many of them. As a rule they advertise very little and generally in genealogical magazines only, such as the *New England Historical and Genealogical Register* or the *American Genealogist*. But there are other ways and means of getting in touch with them. If the librarian of your public library does not know any locally, the curators of the genealogical collections in the larger cities may have a list. Or write to the Board for the Certification of Genealogists, sponsored by the American Society of Genealogists, for an up-to-date list of certified genealogists, American lineage specialists, and genealogical record searchers. The address is 1307 New Hampshire Avenue, N.W., Washington, D.C. 20036. You should remember that a capable genealogist, like any other competent professional man or woman, has spent a great deal of time and money acquiring competency to solve difficult problems. So do not be surprised if a genealogist's fee seems rather stiff. As a matter of fact, it is extremely difficult to fix an equitable charge for any professional service—try to figure out what your own experience in your own line of work is really worth. When you pay a physician, a lawyer, an architect, you are paying for accumulated wisdom and expert knowledge. The same is true when you pay an experienced genealogist. Further, you must realize that no one can guarantee you a solution to your problem (I've been searching half a century for my great-great-grandmother Azubah Doane).

In the interest of accuracy, from the very start beware of using books which are made up of pedigrees and biographical sketches contributed by those who subscribe to the books, sometimes called "mug" books—many reproduce photographs of the biographees. Some of these are good and some of them are bad, but all have to be used with care, and every detail in the lineage must be checked against original records if possible. Until you have done this, you cannot be sure of their reliability. Some of the contributors to such volumes have undoubtedly been very careful in what they supplied, but others have pieced together their pedigrees from unauthentic sources, or guessed at the connecting links. During the last hundred years a great many books of this kind have been published; they are to be found in every genealogical library. As you become familiar with the methods of genealogical research, you will learn to pick the flaws in them and to use them with discretion.

Searching for Your Ancestors is based largely on my own experience gained over a period of more than fifty years. Preconditioned by listening to my grandmother and her sisters talk about their many relations, I was inoculated with the genealogical "bug" by the chance remark of a college classmate. My interest came to life and has never died out: indeed, it has grown as the years have passed. So, if throughout this volume there seem to be too many examples from my personal experience, I hope for forgiveness. Digging for ancestors, like fishing, is a personal matter, and the genealogist, like the sportsman, is always telling stories of his own exploits as you will soon find yourself doing if you become interested in the pursuit.

In this fourth edition of *Searching for Your Ancestors,* I have revised some of the statements made in the earlier editions which are now out of date, corrected some errors, and added some new material.

It is impossible for me to acknowledge all my debts in connection with this book, but I do want to record a few of the greater ones. First, the book itself is due largely to the forbearance of my wife and children in spending a hot summer in Nebraska with me and shielding me from the telephone and other modern conveniences while the text was written. In each successive revision, including this one, there has been an additional period during which I have not been easy to live with!

To the late Donald Lines Jacobus, I owe an intangible debt, for I have gained much from his precepts and his published works.

To the late Mary Walton Ferris, of Chicago, I owe another one of those debts which must always remain unpaid because there is no adequate return for the wisdom which she brought to her consideration of genealogical problems and shared with me. Her book, *The Dawes-Gates Ancestral Lines* (2 vols., 1931, 1943), an outstanding example of the finest type of genealogical work, displays her scholarly ability and the quality of her mind.

For this edition, Stanley Perin, of Marion, Ind., has given me permission to paraphrase and condense his account of his search for the Indian great-great-great-grandmother he was told he had. I hope you will read his article about it, for it is an excellent example of ancestor hunting at its best.

To Alex Haley I am deeply indebted for his account of his experiences in verifying his grandmother's account of the history of her family and his success in tracing it back at least nine generations from clues which she gave him when he was a boy. He has opened up a new field of research, and I look forward with eager interest to his forthcoming book, *Roots.*

To those of you who read this book and are thereby led into the pursuit of your ancestors I owe both congratulations and condolences: condolences because I know that you will never be able to rid yourselves of the desire to search out one more line; and congratulations, because I know that you will have found an absorbing hobby which will profit you in many ways.

And so, good hunting!

G. H. D.

Lincoln, Nebraska, Summer 1936
Newport, Rhode Island, Fall 1972

Contents

CHAPTER ONE

Jaunts and Jollities among Ancestors

"WHO WAS your great-grandmother? What was her maiden name? Where did she live?

If in the last census the enumerator had asked these questions of everyone, and the results had been tabulated, I'll wager the percentage of people who could give the answers would have been small indeed.

Yet an eighth of the blood flowing in your veins came from your great-grandmother, and possibly a much larger proportion of your individual traits: your sweet winning ways or your irascible disposition. Despite loose talk concerning the importance of heredity, we do "take after" people. I know of a woman who lived in one of the New England states during the first half of the nineteenth century. She was noted for her temper and strength of will. By her first husband she had an only child, a son, who married and fathered a large family. Among his children two of the brothers fell into a dispute over some property and lived in the same small village for twenty years afterward without speaking to each other; two of the sisters "got mad" over something or other and refused to recognize each other again. When one of them died, thirty-five years later, the other deliberately mopped her own front porch while the deceased sister's funeral procession was passing! The same pertinacity cropped out in two of that same woman's grandchildren (brothers again) by her second husband.

Do you have a full quota of 1024 great-great-great-great-great-great-great-grandparents in the tenth generation back, or are you, like most of us, a cousin of your

1

own a few times? Are you one of those really rare individuals who can trace descent from every one of the fifty passengers on the *Mayflower* in 1620 from whom a blood descent has been proved, or merely one of the thousands living today who can trace a line back to one or two of that little band? Can you follow your ancestry to a fine old Cavalier family in Virginia, or are you stymied by one of your forefathers who dropped, apparently from heaven, into southern Ohio about 1820? Did this man quarrel with his older brother over the distribution of their father's estate, go west in a huff, change his patronymic, and never mention his rightful name again? A friend of mine has this very problem to solve, and it is a very difficult one.

Have you ever tried to verify the traditions which have been handed down from generation to generation in your family, say that of the seven brothers who came from England in the *Lion's Whelp*? If your name happens to be Allen and your father told you that his father said that he was a descendant of the famous and impetuous Green Mountain Boy, Ethan Allen, have you ever attempted to confirm that statement from the records? Do you know that this particular Ethan Allen had but one living male descendant of the surname Allen in 1900, and hence descent is possible in the female line only? Or did your father say that his father told him that he *thought* the family was related to the Vermont hero?

The Centennial Exposition in Philadelphia in 1876 awakened an interest in the part played in the American Revolution and the establishment of the United States by the grandparents and great-grandparents of those whose awareness of history was thereby stimulated. This, in turn, sparked the founding of the Society of the Daughters of the American Revolution (D.A.R.) in 1890 by a group of patriotic women who wanted to record the service of their progenitors and their own descent from the "fathers of our country." Other societies based on lineal descent, such as the Society of Mayflower Descendants (1897), were engendered and grew apace. Their expanding membership created a continuing interest in family history and tracing descents from more remote progenitors. Hence the development of genealogy as a discipline in this country. Since World War II, the establishment of the five-day week, the expansion of Social Security benefits, and enforced retirement soon after the "prime of life" is presumed to have waned have created a new leisure class. Many in that category have turned to genealogy as something more than a hobby; it becomes an engrossing occupation, a new vocation for an active and inquisitive mind. There are some who, having acquired competence through the years of pursuit when it was an avocation, have been able to eke out inadequate annuities by capitalizing on the expertise they have gained.

Digging for lost ancestors is far more than simply collecting the names of your ascendants. It sometimes takes you into strange places, and in the course of your excavations a considerable amount of history, geography, psychology, and law very likely will be added to your store of knowledge. You don't dig merely to accumulate a lot of dry bones, as it were. Or to change the metaphor, you simply cannot back-trail your progenitors without becoming interested in the times in which they lived and in the various phases of their lives and activities. Suppose you are a midwesterner and are tracing your line of ascent back to the emigrant. You find that your grandfather came to Kansas or Nebraska as a homesteader. If you are not apathetic to the past, you cannot help delving into the history of the famous Homestead Act and learning its effect on the migration to the Great Plains after the Civil War. You go back further and find that your great-grandfather came to Ohio from "York State" and you wonder how they traveled in those days. You dig into the history of the great westward movement which followed the War of 1812 and the building of the Erie Canal, and perhaps you reread *Rome Haul* or *Drums along the Mohawk* with excited interest because now you know that that was the life which your own people lived and knew, or you see some of the historical movies or "documentaries" with greater interest, picturing your own ancestors in them. Then you go back another generation or so and learn that another ancestor took part in the capture of Ticonderoga in 1776 and was one of the Green Mountain Boys. Suddenly all the glamour of that exploit of Ethan Allen's assumes an intimate meaning for you, for a man of your blood was with him and may even have heard the actual words which he used as he demanded the surrender of the fort from the British officer who was nervously clutching his trousers in the dim, cold morning light—a remark probably much more profane than the reputed "Open in the name of the Great Jehovah and the Continental Congress!" It isn't so difficult to visualize such events when you know that your own people took part in them. And incidentally you'll probably observe that in the wake of every war in our history there has developed a restlessness and dis-satisfaction with life as it had been before the war, and that a great movement of people has resulted in each case.

Thus, step by step, generation by generation, you trace the blood back into the past, ultimately reaching the sea-board and the emigrant ancestor. You may be one of those fortunate enough to find records which take the line across the ocean to the "old country." Such a dis-covery, or the effort to make it, frequently results in a clearer understanding of the problems in the Europe of that time, or at least stimulates a desire to know more about it. Possibly you will get from the library Trevel-yan's *England under the Stuarts*, that very readable his-tory of the England from which our forefathers came in the seventeenth century. After reading it you may be interested to go on and trace the parallel development of the democratic idea in the two countries, England and America, and contrast the present-day results.

In riding this hobby you can easily see what fascinat-ing byways there are, lanes which look so inviting that you cannot proceed without investigating them a bit. Consequently, you turn your hobby horse's head away from the main trail and explore a little, knowing that you can always come back again and continue along the main road. Let us suppose that one of your ancestors was a cloth manufacturer in central New York. Doesn't the his-tory of that trade interest you, and aren't you keen to find out what economic conditions caused the family to give up and move westward? Or, again, maybe one of them was a potter and helped to make what is known as Bennington pottery. Now that funny-looking old brown china dog, which Grandmother insisted on lugging out to Iowa with her, comes to mean something, and perhaps you delve into Spargo's book to learn about its manufacture.

Or what if you come upon the rather unsavory fact that your great-great-grandfather was killed by a revenue officer in a raid on the smugglers on Lake Champlain? Are you going to give up digging because you've struck such a rock? Or are you going to look into the history of smuggling in northern Vermont around 1800? If you decide to take up the spade again you will find that many of those people on the border—then truly frontier—had the courage to earn the best living they could and to sell their produce where it would bring them the best return. You'll find that they had many admirable qualities, and were people to be proud of, in spite of their apparent lawlessness.

All this and more will fascinate you. The Cumberland Gap will become more than a railway pass through the Allegheny range if your people came through it before the Baltimore and Ohio Railroad was built. The "State of Frankland" will be more than a mere phrase in a school-book if your people chanced to settle in Tennessee about 1780. "Natchez Trace" will cease to be a mysterious term when you follow your ancestors in their migration from the Carolinas to Louisiana and Texas. History will become part and parcel of your blood.

Even religion may assume a new aspect, or your respect for it may be increased. Suppose that you find you are descended from Mary Dyer, the "Quaker Martyr," who was hanged in Boston, 1 June 1660. Wouldn't you want to know the reason for her fate? There is a saying among her descendants that they are all close-mouthed because she talked too much and got herself hanged. If you find that your family moved from Dartmouth, Mass., to Nine Partners, Dutchess County, N.Y., won't you want to know why there was a migration across Connecticut about 1735, and, moreover, why any town should have been called "Nine Partners"? You'll find that a large group of people who had become Quakers wanted to get away from the rather severe and unpleasant ostracism of the predominating religious element in Massachusetts and have a place of their own, where they could worship as they pleased (and, perhaps, enforce their own ideas of religious belief). You'll learn the history of the grants in Dutchess County and perhaps find your family located in that curiously named area, the Oblong, no longer on the map. You may learn of the rise of the Hicksites, a group of Quakers who seceded from the main body of that faith and followed Elias Hicks, many of them moving westward into Kentucky and southern Ohio. You will run into a hundred and one other sects, each centered around some picturesque leader, such as Mother Ann.

Possibly your people became Mormons and followed Joseph Smith to Nauvoo, Ill., and later accompanied Brigham Young across the Plains to found Salt Lake City and the Mormon empire beyond the Rockies. After a visit to Salt Lake and to what is perhaps the most magnificent location for a city in the entire United States, admiration for the vision of the great Mormon leader grows apace.

Your interest in economic conditions in the past will develop amazingly as you explore. If you have a strain of Irish blood, you will find yourself investigating the great potato famine in Ireland in the 1840's, or going further back and delving into life in Ireland in the seventeenth century, for there was a migration from Ireland to America as early as that. You begin to understand the difference between Ulster and "Ireland," the north and the south of the Emerald Isle, the Orangemen and the wearers of the green.

If your people are of Pennsylvania German ancestry, you may want to dig into the history of the Palatinate in the eighteenth century and find out why there was a great migration from Germany to Pennsylvania in the first half of that period. Then you will discover along what paths those people moved on, southward into Maryland and Virginia, and later westward over the mountains and through the Ohio valley.

Perhaps you have a Huguenot line of descent. What was the history of that famous persecution? What were the conditions in France which caused a whole body of people to flee, first to England, and afterwards to America? Where did they settle?

How long have there been Jews resident in America? Do you know about Judah Touro, that fine old patriarch whose remains lie in a wistaria-draped cemetery on Touro Street in Newport, R.I.? Does the name Abraham Redwood mean anything to you, and are you aware that the oldest library building in America, Redwood Library in Newport, was founded by him in 1752? This library, still a "subscription library," is located on Bellevue Avenue, one of the most noted streets in America, on which are to be found the summer villas of the Vanderbilts, Astors, and Whitneys. In front of it stands the first fern beech to be transplanted from Switzerland to America, a truly beautiful tree, well worth traveling to see in its lacy beauty on a bright summer day.

These are but a few of the fascinating byways of genealogy. The average scoffer does not realize that digging for ancestors means far more than merely accumulating names. He thinks of it as "dry as dust" and even less interesting. He does not understand that it is a stimulating, living study, well worth pursuing, and that from it we may learn not only the history of our own family but also a great deal about the history of our country in which our own people have played a part.

Genealogical research doesn't call for a lot of expensive equipment—just a notebook, a few pencils, an inquisitive mind, and a willingness to ask questions and dig for facts. You must gather what you can from relatives; the older they are, the better. Incidentally, there are sometimes unexpected profits in paying a little attention to them. One ancestor hunter received a legacy from a distant relative whom she knew only by correspondence, simply because she had shown an interest in the history of the family and thus pleased the old lady.

But all that comes to you from Great-Aunt Hettie, or garrulous Uncle Abijah, must not be accepted as the truth. The memories of some old folks are less reliable than those of others. Some like to make a good story out of a fact; some do not realize how much they have forgotten and how much they have added to the story in telling it. Your job is to note the details as best you can and check them later.

Once the memory of your older relatives is exhausted, you begin to dig in official records: vital records, probate records, church records, and the like. Each yields its quota of amusement, as well as information, as does the following from the East Haddam, Conn., land records:

> John the sone of John Warner and of Mahittabel his wife was borne December ye: 18th: 1716
>
> Daniell ye sone of John Warnor and of Mahittabell his wife was borne May ye: 6th: 1717

To this the editor of the printed records has added the pertinent comment, "Quick work!"

Cemeteries, too, contain many things both puzzling and droll. I found a stone in a northern Vermont cemetery on which the inscription had been completely defaced. What is the story behind that vandalism? In the same cemetery I found the following inscription:

> Sacred to the Memory of Inestimable Worth to Unrivaled Excellence and Virtue, Miss Cynthia Page, Whose Remains are Deposited here and Whose Ethereal Part Became a Seraph on the 4th of March 1824—Aged 20 Years.

Nearby lies:

> Diah Sherwood, Died April 24, 1853, in his 90th Year. A Soldier of the Revolution

and beside him:

> Jayhannah, wife of Dyer Sherwood, Died May 22, 1833, in Her 67th Year

What a task I had identifying "Diah" or "Dyer"! Alas for the New Englander's propensity for attaching "r" to words ending in a vowel sound. After several years of searching I finally discovered that "Dyer" (as his name was spelled in most of the land records pertaining to him) was identical with Jedediah Sherwood, who migrated from Connecticut to Vermont about 1790, later moved to Ohio, and finally returned to Vermont, where he died.

Wills, too, are more than records of bequests and disposals. In a certain probate court there is a pre-Revolutionary will in which the testator specified the actual rooms in his house which each of his two daughters and his widow were to have after his death. Each was to have right of way through the central hallway and across the garden to the well. It is easy to picture the family: a thrice-married man who at death was survived by a daughter of each of his first two wives and by his third wife. With each of the three women jealous of the other two, the old man was wise enough to know that there would be an unholy scramble, once he was gone, unless he made explicit terms in his bequest.

Sometimes the digger for ancestors is fortunate enough to find a printed genealogy of the family into which he has traced his line of ascent. These records must always be checked for accuracy, and not followed blindly. Occasionally humorous elements are found in them—another proof of my contention that genealogy is not dry. In the Dewey genealogy one comes across this amazing collection of names in one family:

Armenius Philadelphus
Almira Melpomena
Pleiades Arastarcus
Victor Millenius
Octavia Ammonia

and last of all:

Encyclopedia Britannica

The last-named, the compiler states, was living unmarried at the age of 84. I am not surprised at her spinsterhood, for what man would want to marry an encyclopedia?

What a record is found on page 62 of *The Daniel Shed Genealogy*! There it is stated that Ebenezer Richardson, born in Billerica, Mass., 2 October 1724, married, first, Elizabeth Shed, who bore him ten children and died about 1763. He married, secondly, in October 1764, Mary Crosby, who died before 1770, for in December of that year he married, thirdly, Mrs. Lydia Danforth. She died, and he married, fourthly, in December 1776, Mrs. Catherine Wyman. She succumbed, and he married, fifthly, in May 1783, Elizabeth Bacon. She died, and he married, sixthly, Mrs. Susanne Davis, who died. In October 1799, he married, seventhly, Mrs. Keziah Wyman. As the compiler states, "after a long life, rich in marital experience, he succumbed in 1808 to the fell destroyer that had bereft him of so many wives."

The pension records of the survivors of the Revolutionary War not only yield a great store of genealogical data and military records, but present their problems as well. In one such record there was found an affidavit stating that the soldier had married in Paris, Me., and removed to "Thunderstood," Vt. No atlas of Vermont ever noted such a place. It proved to be an old lady's mispronunciation and phonetic spelling of Hungerford, now Sheldon, Vt.

Incidentally, the early census takers were marvels when it came to spelling, for in the first federal census, of 1790, we find the surname Reynolds spelled in thirty-four different ways, ranging from Ranals through Renholds, Reynull, and a few other spellings to Runnels and Rynolds. They managed to spell even Brown in seven ways: Bronn, Broons, Broun, Broune, Brown, Browne, and Brownes! Possibly some of this misspelling in the printed transcript is due to difficulty in reading the old handwriting, for it is hard to read, especially if the paper has become time-stained or the ink has been exposed to the light.

The peculiarities of handwriting are of infinite variety. Searl has been read Scant, and some genealogists have been led along a false trail as a result. At intervals over several years I have been hunting in a Vermont town, and each time I have been there I have taken one more look at a particularly obscure record in the town books. It is a marriage record on which the ancestry of the grandmother of a friend of mine depends. We have been unable to determine whether her name was Monroe or Morris. It happens that neither family is known in that neighborhood. Since the lady whose identity is sought was a widow, it is possible that she was visiting relatives when she met and married as his fifth wife the man who was her second husband.

Speaking of surnames, here is another absorbing byway of genealogical study: the history and development of names. When William the Conqueror established himself in England surnames were almost unknown, even among noble, baronial families. They were not generally adopted until the thirteenth century or later. Most English surnames are derived from names of places or occupations, and a few from some peculiar trait or nickname. For example, the surname Atwood is derived from Atte Wood, that is, John Atte Wood, or John who lived at, or by, the wood, to distinguish him from John Atte Lea (now Atleigh, or more simply Lee), John who lived by the meadow. From these examples it is easy to see how the spelling has gradually simplified until the names have assumed the form with which we are familiar today. Sherman is an occupational name, meaning "shear man," one who sheared cloth. Chandler derives from candlemaker; Thatcher from roof-thatcher. Names derived from places generally had the French preposition *de* inserted between the given name and the surname. For instance, the earliest occurrence of the name Hungerford as applied to an individual is that of Everard de Hungerford, who lived at Hungerford in Berkshire in the twelfth century. By 1500 the *de* had been dropped and the Hungerford family was well established. Seymour is a phonetic spelling of Saint Maur, with a few elisions, thus "de Saint Maur" became Seymour in the course of a few generations. Powell is a corruption of Ap Howell, a Welsh name signifying "son of Howell." Price was originally Ap Rhys, "son of Rhys," a common Welsh given name. Thistlethwaite comes from two words: thistle and thwaite, the last an Anglo-Saxon word meaning "parcel of land" (thistle patch, as we might say). Smith, the most common name, is occupational in origin—William the Smith, to distinguish him from William the Thatcher.

Thus it is easy to see that families of the same surname are not necessarily of the same common stock or origin. Smiths were common throughout England, hence the name had its origin in almost any hamlet in England. But occasionally a name is so unusual that you are justified in assuming that all people of that name living today are related in some degree. However, this is not invariably true, for such a name as Cobleigh when analyzed yields two words "cob" and "leigh," that is, a "roundish lump" and a "meadow." Many a parish might have a field in which there was a rise of ground, and hence that name might originate in several different parts of England. (See Chapter Thirteen for a further note on names.)

There may be some who still persist in wanting to know: "Now, why all this fuss about genealogy? Of what use is it?" One might as well ask: "Of what use postage stamps, Sandwich glass, Currier and Ives prints, match-packet covers?" In the first place, it can be a hobby, an avocation. Psychologists tell us that it is good for a man to have a hobby on which to spend his spare time, something to study, something in the pursuit of which he can broaden his knowledge of the world and its ways. Genealogy is the study of family origins and the ways of individuals; individuals and families help to make history. The late Dr. LeRoy Crummer used to insist that "every man should study the past in order to understand the present and anticipate the future." The doctor applied that maxim to the study of medical history, but it is equally applicable to any other field. Also, individuals make up towns, towns make up counties and states, states make up nations, and nations make up the world and play an important part in its affairs. Thus, in the first or the last analysis, the individual counts.

All in all, you cannot escape the fact that your ascendants were human beings, not merely names which have survived in musty old records. They lived and breathed, had their joys and pleasures, their trials and tribulations, their work and play, however different these may have been from yours. Moreover you will find that they, obscurely or prominently, took their part in the affairs of their times and contributed in some way to the development of civilization. By learning more about them and their times, you'll be the wiser in knowing "how we got this way."

CHAPTER TWO

How to Search among the Relatives

IF YOU really want to dig for your ancestors and have determined to learn something about your progenitors and ascendants, the material equipment is very slight. You needn't buy a lot of tools—spades, fishing tackle, clubs—or a horse. As I have said, all you'll need is a good notebook, preferably loose-leaf, of a size convenient to carry. Don't make the mistake of getting one that is too small, or one that holds only a few sheets of paper. I think you will find it best to have a page at least five and a half by eight and a half inches (I like the size taking a standard sheet of typewriter paper, eight and a half by eleven). I recommend, also, one that opens like a book rather than one opening at the end. If your notebook is hinged along the side you can extend your pedigree charts across two pages, and thus be able to see a whole "line" without turning a page. I prefer the larger sized notebook, also, because I can put into it letters and other typewritten papers by simply punching the proper holes and inserting the sheets wherever I want them. A supplementary working notebook of pocket size is useful when you begin to take trips. Indeed, some genealogists always carry about with them such a notebook in which they keep notes of the details wanted on specific problems. My own "traveling" notebook, always in my bag when I go to libraries or other places where I am likely to find records, contains sheet after sheet on which are noted problems in my own ancestry still unsolved and a few of those on which my friends are working.

Before beginning to question one's relatives, it is well

to prepare an ancestral chart or skeleton outline of your ancestry. Such a chart can be made easily with a pencil and ruler on a sheet of your notebook paper—at least that is the way I usually make them for working purposes; see Form 1 (page 15). A similar one, printed on standard size typewriter paper, can be obtained from Goodspeed's Book Shop, 18 Beacon Street, Boston, Mass. 02108, or other firms dealing in genealogical supplies. You can begin with your own name—if you propose to work out both paternal and maternal ancestry—on the single line of the left-hand side of this chart. On the upper of the next two horizontal lines, write your father's full name (start out right and never use an initial when you can get the full name), and immediately below it enter the place and date of his birth, the place and date of his marriage, and the place and date of his death (if he is not living). On the lower enter your mother's full maiden name. In the next column you will note that there are four horizontal lines, on and under which should be recorded the same data for your grandparents. Always record the wives under their maiden names, for in the next generation those become the names of the lines which you are tracing. In the fourth column are spaces for your eight great-grandparents. Thus, on a single chart, when all the spaces are filled out, you will have the data on four generations, including yourself, if you have started with your own name.

You will notice the legend "Chart No. 1" in the upper right-hand corner of Form 1. If you look carefully, you will see that a number of two digits follows each of the eight "great-grandparent" spaces. This number refers to the chart on which that individual's line is carried along. To continue this line, let us say your paternal grandmother's paternal line, you start another chart, placing on the single line at the left-hand side the name of that great-grandfather; just as you have filled out Chart 1, you fill out his ancestry on this new chart, which gets its number, 13, from the number following his name on Chart 1. Thus this new chart becomes Chart 13. You may wonder why the numbers 2 to 10, inclusive, have been skipped. It is a little difficult to explain, but I'll try to make it clear.

Chart No. 1

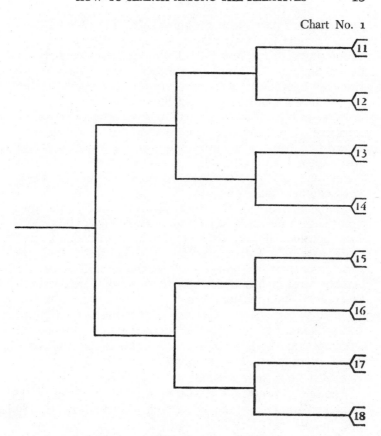

FORM 1. Skeletal Ancestral Chart.

If the charts are numbered consecutively, 1, 2, 3, etc., it is necessary to figure out the whole number of charts that will be needed when a particular ancestry is complete. But, as it is seldom possible to work out all the lines immediately, I find it easier to use a system enabling me to insert new charts at any place at any time. So, after renumbering my charts many times, I hit upon this system of numbering. Calling my first outline Chart 1, I then take that number and add to it the digit representing whichever great-grandparent is carried forward. Thus my father's mother's father comes on the third line in the right-hand column, and his chart gets the number 1 plus the digit 3, or 13. If I have carried out this great-grandfather's paternal line, that is, his great-grandfather's line, the next chart gets the number 131, that is, 13 plus 1, representing the first line at the right of that chart. If, at a later date, the mother's mother's line is worked out the new chart has the number 17 and is inserted in the loose-leaf notebook following Chart 13.

Another type of chart showing a skeleton of a complete ancestry, called the radial or semicircular chart, is illustrated in Form 2. It may be drawn in full circle, one-half for paternal and one-half for maternal ancestry. This type, too, can be either purchased or drawn by hand with compass and ruler.

At the foot, or on the back, of each chart you should record the sources of your information for each generation because, if you or any of your descendants ever want to join a patriotic society such as the D.A.R., or any other organization in which one qualification for membership is based on heredity, you will need those references. As a matter of fact, since genealogy is a type of history, the history of an individual family, and since history should always be documented with references to sources, you should get into the habit of noting references in order that you may easily recheck your data should the occasion demand it.

Another, simple type of skeleton chart or record is the pedigree, shown as Form 3 on page 50, which gives only one line of descent. The angled rules show the "blood line" from the earliest known progenitor of the author of this book in his patrilineal line. This same type may be used to indicate the line of descent from any other ancestor, such as your mother's great-grandfather on her mother's side, who, let us say, was one of the founders and first settlers of the town in which she was born and lived until she married your father, a descent in which she took considerable pride and therefore she gave you his name. Remember that the "blood line" should always indicate the person through whom the descent is carried down; hence it may go through the wife instead of the husband in some generations.

Now, with this preliminary excursion into dull directions ended, let us push on to our digging. With your

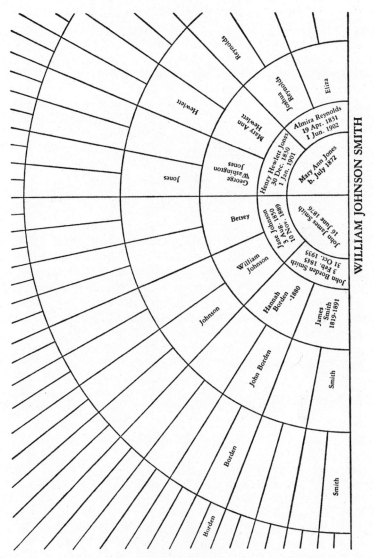

FORM 2. Radial Chart Showing Spaces for Six Generations of Ancestors.

trusty notebook in hand, and a pocketful of good sharp pencils, I suggest that you begin the rounds of the relatives who live within calling distance. If any of your grandparents are alive, that is the best starting point for this peregrination of consanguinity. Let us suppose that your father's father, your grandfather, is the first whom you visit. Most people of his generation enjoy telling a younger person about their own times, which almost invariably seem better to them than those in which we are living! So, it ought to be easy to get him started on his reminiscences. The machinery of memory may creak a little at first, but as he gets into thinking about it, and you go back to see him again and again, he'll probably recall more and more of the details which you need for your history of the family.

He will surely be able to give you the names of his parents—your great-grandparents—and the names of his grandparents, and he may even remember the name of a great-grandparent or two; and you will thus have five generations of ancestors. He may remember where most of these people lived or died. Don't let him off with simply given names or nicknames if he can possibly remember full names and proper names. If he says that his mother's name was Patty, try to find out whether it was actually Patty, or really Martha, Patience, or Patricia (Patty is used as a nickname, or diminutive, for all three). Incidentally, to illustrate my point, one of my friends had a difficult time determining the parentage of one of her great-grandmothers whose name was reported to her to be Patty Cobb. The name proved to be Martha Cobb in the birth record, although she had always been called "Patty." Thus, for further search, in the event that your grandfather doesn't recall his grandmother's parentage, it is essential to know just what her full name was, as well as what she was familiarly called. Nicknames, or "pet" names, are sometimes given in parentheses or square brackets, so you can have the record of both.

Try to get your grandfather to remember and tell you as many dates and names of places as he can. Although at first you may be interested in tracing your paternal line only, you will become interested, undoubtedly, in all lines sooner or later, so it is just as well to make note of everything Grandfather tells you. Thus, if he knows the names of his mother's parents, get them while you can. I recall that, when I was questioning my grandfather about his mother's people—for I started on that line rather than on any of my paternal lines, in response to a query from a genealogist who was compiling a history of that family—just out of politeness (or perhaps in response to some subconscious hunch), I asked him to tell me the names of the parents of his father, and what his grandmother's maiden name was. He told me that he thought she was born a Sherwood (she had died several years before he was born). It was a fortunate question, for after his death a year or two later, that slight clue was all I had as a starting point from which to work out that line, since I could not find in the official town records any mention of my great-great-grandfather's marriage.

My own experience in this matter indicates how important it is to get as much information as you can from old people while you are talking with them. They have a positive genius for dying just before you decide to go back to them for further information. Had I waited until I became interested in tracing my entire ancestry, the only source of information about a starting point on this particular line would have passed beyond my reach. "Gather ye rosebuds while ye may" is a good motto for an ancestor hunter. It is infinitely better to have too much information than not enough.

Always take notes as you talk with your relatives. Otherwise little details, which are frequently of importance to you in your pursuit of the elusive ancestor, may escape you, and you'll find yourself wishing that you had made more careful notes. If you are not sure of a point ask about it again, or put a question mark after your note in order that you may verify it more completely later.

Let us suppose that Grandfather says that his father was born in Postville, Ill., 2 July 1863, and tells you that his grandfather was fighting at the Battle of Gettysburg on that day and did not know his eldest son was born until several weeks later, because the letter giving the news did not reach him, owing to the movement of the troops. Moreover, since his grandfather was at war, his grandmother was living with her parents. This is all interesting and may furnish you with some facts which shed a light on the history of the family. As he talks, he tells you that his grandparents had a pretty hard time to get along after his grandfather returned from the war, and that his father was four years old when the next child, his sister, was born in a covered wagon as they were crossing Iowa. Following up this lead, you question him further about the reason for the move and learn that his grandfather, as a soldier, located a homestead in Nebraska under the Homestead Act, which Congress passed in 1862.

As Grandfather has been talking you have filled in some of the spaces on your working chart, and the blank pages following it have been filling up with notes which you can later expand into a narrative account of the family. Now you might get him to tell you the names of his brothers and sisters and give you their birth dates or, at least, the order of their births and the names of the places where they were born. Perhaps he will remember the names of paternal or maternal uncles and aunts, and some details of their lives. These data aren't essential to you, but they help to complete the picture of the family (and may enable you later to help some cousin work out a line). If he says that his Uncle Harry disappeared and that the last the family heard of him he was with Custer in the Sioux Wars, record that fact, and later, if you wish, look up the history of Custer's campaign and the famous battle of Little Big Horn River.

Perhaps Grandfather's father lost his life in the great blizzard of 12 January 1888, in Nebraska, and about 1893 his mother married again, say a widower on a neighboring farm. His stepfather's name and any details about possible half brothers and sisters will help to make the story more interesting and complete.

As a matter of fact, while you are talking with older relatives, it is always wise to get the names of brothers and sisters (whole or half) as well as aunts and uncles, and names of their children. Sometimes recollections are handed down or remembered in one branch of the family which have been forgotten (if ever known) in another.

One of my correspondents remembered that his grand-father had a brother. The official death record of the grandfather did not show the names of his parents and gave only New York as his place of birth; that of his great-uncle gave all their names and the town which enabled him to trace his paternal ancestry back to the immigrant three centuries ago.

The chances are that there are interesting anecdotes about the various migrations of the family, if they moved about at all. One of my friends told me that her grand-father was a baby when the family moved from western New York to Ohio and, as they were traveling to Buffalo to get the boat on which they were to go up Lake Erie to their new home, he, sleeping in the end of the bob-sled in which they were traveling, rolled off and wasn't missed for a mile or so!

Possibly the story is entirely different and your grand-father was a bound boy and came from Michigan. In that case, urge him to recall as much as possible about him-self: whether he came out of an orphanage or was bound out by his mother because his father was killed in the Civil War and she couldn't take care of him. Such a case presents a difficult problem but not necessarily an in-soluble one. Local records of the community in which his foster parents lived may show something, if he re-members where they lived and who they were. Their blood descendants may recall details which he has for-gotten. Orphanage records may show where he came from or who his parents were. Ask him to characterize his parents and tell you any traditions about his family. Although you yourself may not belong to any church or be of a religious turn of mind, don't forget that church records are a source of valuable information. He should also tell you to what church his family belonged; you can later try to find its records.

All such details should be noted down. But a word of caution about these questions: don't try to get too much information at any one time. Remember that old folks tire easily. Cultivate them and let them do most of the talking, and don't attempt to confine them to any one line of talk. One detail leads to another. As they turn over in their minds the incidents of their lives, more and

more comes back to them. A forgotten detail is sometimes recalled the next day or later. I know of one case
in which an elderly man was repeatedly asked for information regarding his grandfather in the hope that a clue
to his identity and occupation might be obtained. Finally,
one day, a chance remark "rang a bell" and brought out
the whole story with a wealth of detail.

If there are any other relatives alive, get their addresses and begin a correspondence with them. Check
the details received from one against those from another.
Note the discrepancies, as well as the coincidences, and
try to sift the facts as you go along. It is sometimes very
difficult to reconcile statements made by different members of the family, but generally there is an element of
truth somewhere. What an old person recalls about one
member of the family may properly apply to someone
else, only the names have been mixed.

Sometimes old friends of the family, living in the community from which they came, can supply the missing
data. One very interesting case has come to my attention. A friend was trying to prove his wife's descent from
a passenger on the *Mayflower* to secure for her membership in the Society of Mayflower Descendants. Although
she knew her grandmother's parentage, they could not
find a single record to prove it. They knew that this
woman's father had lived in a certain town in Connecticut, but that she had actually been born in Vermont or
New Hampshire and raised by her mother's relatives,
since her mother died soon after her birth. The records
of Canterbury, Conn., indicate that her father died unmarried. That was a hard hurdle to take. But, by going
back to Connecticut and talking with the old men in that
town, they found one who had been the lifelong chum
of this great-grandfather—a very old man fortunately
possessing a clear mind and memory. He said that he
was about the only person who knew that Septus Ens-
worth had gone away as a young man, that he had met a
girl and married her, and that she had died at the birth
of their child a year later. Brokenhearted, he left his
baby daughter with his wife's family in Vermont and
returned to his native town in Connecticut, where he
died at an advanced age without ever seeing his daughter

again. He never remarried, and, in order not to be reminded of his sorrow, hadn't talked about his early marriage except to this one very close friend. The old man, whom my friends had found, made an affidavit about these details before a notary public. With this as documentation, the line of descent was accepted and my friend's wife was admitted to the society. Two years later they went back again to see the old man, but he had died very suddenly just a month after they had met him!

This incident again shows that you must dig while the weather is good or the circumstances permit, and leave no stone unturned.

Whenever possible, it is best to talk with old people in person, for they find it difficult to write letters, especially if there are many details. In talking person to person, one question leads to another, or a chance remark leads to further queries and brings out information which they wouldn't think of writing down. Alert for facts, you can seize upon a slight clue and get them to elaborate it in conversation, but this is difficult to do in correspondence. Sometimes, however, geographical distance prevents a personal interview. In this case, make your questions as specific and clear as possible when you are writing. I find it expedient to write out my questions on a separate sheet of paper, leaving spaces for the answers, so they can be filled in on the same sheet, which is to be returned to me and inserted in my notebook. It is always a mark of courtesy, if nothing more, to enclose with your sheet of questions a self-addressed and stamped envelope: this makes it simpler for your correspondent to answer and helps to ensure a reply. Old people find it a task to write letters and so they have a tendency to put off doing it—sometimes until it is too late—so it is best to do all that you can to lighten the chore for them.

I recall that, in the early days of my genealogical experience, I wrote to a great-aunt and asked her to give me the names of the descendants of her grandfather and tell me all she knew about them. Although she was a good correspondent and loved to write letters, she was a little slow in answering this one. Finally, however, I received a reply. She began to enumerate the grandfather's children and tell about their marriages. After she had listed about four of them (he had twelve, this hardy old pioneer!), she wrote: "Oh, this is too much to write. I'll tell you about them sometime." It *was* too much, for when I finally completed the records of all these descendants there were about three hundred of them! Later, when I was able to visit her, she told me much that she did not have the patience to write.

If you can persuade your grandfather, or another older relative, to go to the cemetery with you and explain the relationship that existed between those buried in the family lot or near it, you will often save much time and trouble. Sometimes different generations of the family are buried in different cemeteries. In my own case, my grandparents, great-grandparents, and great-great-grandparents are buried in different cemeteries in the same town. If I hadn't had my great-aunt go the round of those cemeteries with me, and point out the graves of these ancestors, I would have had a great deal of trouble in finding them and securing the data from their gravestones; for there are ten graveyards in that town, and I know it to be a fact that there are over three thousand stones in those yards—I have since copied the inscriptions.

Tact and diplomacy are very necessary in digging among the relatives. I know of one instance in which a problem is practically insoluble without the Bible records which are in the possession of a distant relative of the person interested. The latter has in some manner offended her relative cousin and now is at a standstill in her search, because the possessor of the records ignores her letters. Moreover, that relative is now suspicious of anyone else who tries to gain access to the Bible!

When personal relations are uncertain, it is not politic to demand access to a record, of course, but more diplomatic to play upon the owner's sympathy or to discover some roundabout method of obtaining the information. If you haven't ever "gotten along with" Cousin Emma, why not persuade George, her favorite, to copy those records or get the information which you want? Don't risk a brusque refusal, and at the same time arouse her suspicion that everyone else who may approach her is working at your request. This art of getting along with irascible people is one of the things which you can learn in genealogical work, if you haven't acquired it already.

Another thing which must be handled with tact is the matter of private scandal. You should know all family scandal—not as dirt for dirt's sake, but rather because it is often necessary to the proper carrying on of the investigation. While I was gathering material for a genealogy of my mother's maternal family, I went to a much older cousin for data about her aunts and uncles. She was very reluctant to talk about them, didn't even remember their names! I was surprised, for I had never before detected in her a failing memory. Later, I asked my mother why she wouldn't talk and was told that one of the aunts had been divorced and later sent to a state asylum. So my genealogy was published without a complete record of that branch of the family. When this cousin read it and saw that I did not mention the cause of the divorce she recalled—when it was too late to use them—all the details for which I had asked the year before. If I had known this "scandal" before going to her, I probably would have been able to indicate more clearly the reason for my inquisitiveness and assure her of my discretion in using what she told me. There is no need of raking up too much past scandal, but one should know enough of it to be able to handle such situations tactfully. Moreover, what seemed scandalous fifty years ago is now accepted without batting an eyelash, at least in many circles.

CHAPTER THREE

What about Those Family Traditions?

As I HAVE suggested, don't accept as gospel truth all that your Great-Aunt Hettie, or Uncle Abijah, tells you about the history of the family. Older people do not always realize that they have confused two different episodes and telescoped them into one; and sometimes they do not discriminate between fact and fiction. Some are natural-born storytellers and quite unconsciously embroider the facts a little here and there to make the tale more dramatic, all the while really believing that they are relating the details as they heard them from their grandsire. Others, who give every evidence of a remarkably retentive memory, tell a clear and straightforward account of the family as they received it from an older generation without realizing that the tradition may have been distorted before they heard it.

So listen carefully and attentively to what your elderly relatives pass on to you. Remember, many old people talk more or less at random, skipping back and forth as the wheels of memory begin to turn more easily, or they remember more clearly some detail and go back, without warning, to correct it or add to it. Sometimes they will tell the same story twice, having recollected something they have left out. It is really quite difficult sometimes to follow the thread of their story, so you may have to ask for the connection with what you have already heard.

Make an effort to remember the details as faithfully as you can, especially if you have to trust to your own memory rather than take notes. Your pencil and pad may disconcert an older person as you try to write down details or even key points in the story. Moreover, unless you have had stenographic training, or have learned speedwriting, it is virtually impossible to write fast enough to get down on paper the full story while they are reciting it. If you are lucky enough to own a tape recorder, take it along with you. Uncle 'Bijah may be willing to talk into it, and, when you play back some of it, enjoy listening to his own voice.

Later, the sooner the better, while it is still fresh in your mind, write down what you have heard, or transcribe your notes or your tapes, so you can sort out the details and will not have to depend on your own memory to put in the connecting links.

When you have got all that Aunt Hettie told you arranged in some sort of order, you may want to go back and ask her to tell you more about one point or another. This has a double advantage: your own recollection may be clarified, or she may, by that time, remember names and facts which she left out in her earlier account of it. Names and even dates do sometimes "come to you" hours later—a fact which, as I have discovered in myself now that I am advancing in years, happens quite frequently! Moreover, with the family saga somewhat organized in your own mind, you may well try to get another version of it from Uncle 'Bijah, or at least give him an opportunity to verify it. It is always an advantage if you can get two independent accounts and check to see if they tally. One cousin, aunt, or uncle may remember what another does not recall. The mind of one may retain details which didn't interest the other and were not remembered. By comparing and piecing together two or three independent recollections of the details, you may be able to put together a better history.

Even if accounts do not differ significantly, you must check the details as best you can against such sources as you can find, preferring public records, such as I discuss in another chapter, or any written or printed evidence which you may find. This is especially important before you accept as true what your narrators have told you about an episode which happened before their own time. What a person does not know from his own participation in, or recollection of, a given event is hearsay, not bona fide evidence. Hearsay may be distorted or inaccurate. A mother may tell her daughter the date on which she married that daughter's father, the names of her parents and her husband's parents, as well as the date the daughter was born. Presumably such information is true, but you should make an effort to verify it if possible. When the mother tells her daughter what her father told her about his grandparents or great-grandparents, she is passing on tradition, which may be true, or distorted or erroneous.

Speaking of differences in memory, my own father, fifty years ago when I first quizzed him about his mother's family, could tell me very little about that side of the house. At first, he couldn't recall even the maiden name of his grandmother, his mother's mother, who, to be sure, died when he was a boy; later, having learned her name from his sister, Father remembered some details about his cousins. Fortunately, my father's only sister, fifteen months younger than he, remembered much more about her mother's people (my grandmother lived with my aunt during the last twenty years of her life, so my aunt had much more opportunity to hear those relatives mentioned). From her I got the names of her grandparents, a great-grandfather, several cousins, aunts, and uncles, and a couple of great-aunts, and great-uncles, so I could construct quite a pedigree of that family which I verified from gravestones and public records. From one of the second cousins, a "remove" or two from me, whom I discovered almost by chance. I gleaned even more about our common progenitors. He was, in truth, quite a bit older than my aunt so he remembered some people whom my aunt never mentioned. From his recollections, I learned two interesting and significant details: one, that the great-grandfather of my grandmother, having come from Canada into northern Vermont, spoke French Canadian patois, the language of his childhood, fluently, but quite broken English; and, secondly, that there was Indian blood in the family. When I expressed my interest in the latter, he became confidential, apparently having decided to trust me, and told me quite a gruesome story about a great-great uncle which was really something! When I got the progenitor's pension record from the National Archives—he served in the Revolutionary War —and noted that his birthplace was given as Saint Ours in Lower Canada (now Quebec), the French-speaking tradition seemed verified, at least circumstantially. It wasn't until I found his will in a Vermont probate office that I learned his father's name. Going to Saint Ours, I found no record, civil or ecclesiastical, of either him or his father. I have yet to verify, after half a century of searching, the Indian blood, although the temperaments of some of my grandmother's relations whom I know, if not their physical characteristics, seem to suggest it. The gruesome story is confirmed by an account of religious fanaticism and cruelty found in Crocker's *History of the Baptists in Vermont,* which lends credence to the strain of Indian blood said to have been in the family—at least, I am willing to accept the tradition in the hope that I may yet find more convincing evidence.

This leads me to summarize the experience of a friend who successfully tracked down a similar tradition in his family.

He grew up believing the tradition that was current in his father's family. When he wanted to know the facts, his father told him that his grandmother, Rachel Rice, brought Indian blood into the Perin family. Whenever he had leisure, he studied the family history and began to compile and verify the facts. He tried to study the physiognomy of as many of Rachel's descendants as he could, noting the texture of the hair, the bone structure of the features of uncles, aunts, and cousins of one degree or another. According to Mendel's law, a percentage of them should have had one or more typical Indian traits and characteristics, if the tradition was true. When he found no trace of any Indian features or even a hint of one, he concluded that there was no truth in the tradition, but he still wanted to know how it came about that his father and grandfather believed that there was Indian blood. So he continued his search for the progenitors of Rachel Rice, his great-grandmother. One of his cousins gave him his first clue, which she found in a history of Tompkins County, N.Y. This mentioned the migration of his great-grandparents, John and Rachel Perin, from western Massachusetts to that county. In reading over the chapter, he found that a family with which he had a possible connection was said to have come from Charlemont,

Berkshire County, Mass., so he centered his search there. He soon discovered that Captain Moses Rice was living there when he was killed by the Indians, and his grandson, Asa, was carried away captive. Asa lived with his captors for about six or seven years before he was redeemed at the age of fifteen; therefore, it seemed quite unlikely that he had taken an Indian girl as a mate. Continuing his search, my friend learned that Asa married, not once but twice, white women, and fathered quite a family, among them Rachel, whom he named as Rachel Perin in his will. Thus the tradition of Indian blood was disproved and in its place my friend found that he had a great-great-grandfather who, in his youth, was a captive among the Indians for several years. If you are sufficiently interested in how my friend followed step by step the clues which he picked up along the trail into the past, you will find the full story and the surprising happenstance by which the final, conclusive evidence was found in the *New England Historical and Genealogical Register* (Vol. 121, January 1967, pp. 29–36). The author is Stanley E. Perin; the title "A Tradition in Search of Its Origin." It is not only an exciting story; it is also an excellent example of first-class genealogical research.

So much for one type of tradition. Now I want to discuss the fanciful type.

If the basic fact in the tradition in Mr. Perin's family became distorted in three generations, consider the following letter, which another friend of mine asked me to read about forty years ago. He had written to one of his distant cousins asking her to talk with her aged grandmother about the history of the family and where they had lived before moving to the West. (Note: I no longer have access to the original letter, which I copied verbatim changing only the names, as my friend requested.) It read:

Here is all Grandma can think of about the fore fathers.
Lord John Whiting, Great Grandfather, was born in 1735, near London. He came to America on the May Flower in 1776 soon after the Revolutionary War, bringing his two daughters, Lady Jane and Mabel (Not sure of the name). She, Mabel, went back to England with her father.

Lord Whiting bought some land in Connecticut and gave it to Lady Jane for a wedding present when she married grandfather James Dupey (he was a French nobleman) in 1796 or 1798. James Dupey was Captain of the May Flower. Ten sons were born to them.

I cite this fantastic account simply to point out some of the incongruities which, I trust, will strike you immediately. In fact, you might stop at this point and test your skill in spotting the anachronisms before you read on. Surely most of the school histories of our country still contain an account of the historic voyage of the *Mayflower* overloaded with 102 passengers and all the alleged heirlooms, the date of its arrival, and the horrors of that first winter, 1620–21. Most high school students know that the Revolutionary War was not over until the surrender of Cornwallis at Yorktown in 1781, and that the independence of the United States was not formally recognized until the signing of the Treaty of Paris in 1783. These facts are sufficient to give warning that this story must have been told by an elderly person who had lost quite a few of her buttons. Consequently, it is of almost no value to one searching for ancestors and trying to discover something about the history of his family. The only clue of immediate value lies in the mention of Connecticut as the place of settlement, and there research should be centered once the trail has been followed back to New England. You may be interested to know that my friend found that this was true. Following up some of the distaff families he discovered a line of descent from one of the passengers on the historic *Mayflower*, although the name was not that mentioned by Grandma, and another from a Huguenot who fled from France after the revocation of the Edict of Nantes in 1685 and settled in Connecticut.

In these two examples of family traditions, the one had on the face of it the semblance of truth, but, after careful examination, followed by tracing the pedigree of the great-grandmother involved, proved to be a distortion of fact; the other which seemed to be a figment of the imagination, or at most the tale of one whose mind, perhaps weakened by illness and age, wandered from one vague recollection to another in strange fancy, did have, deeply buried in its fantasy, some basic facts.

There was, however, in the history of our progenitors, a time when oral tradition was remarkably clear and accurate. Pedigrees were memorized and handed on from generation to generation, with appropriate additions in each. There were uncounted examples of such oral pedigrees among the ancient Scandinavians, the Irish, the Welsh, the Scots, the Icelanders, the Maoris in New Zealand, and the native tribes of Africa. In Ireland, for example, for many centuries, the *filid,* or the hereditary historians of the clan, or sept, were trained to memorize and recite, without error or omission, the descent from the "founder" or progenitor, not only of the main stem of the family, but also its agnate branches. In Iceland, there were handed down from generation to generation lines of descent from the first settlers who came across the sea from Scandinavia in the ninth century to colonize that uninhabited island. These pedigrees were not written down until the twelfth century when Ari Thorgilsson compiled the *Landnamabok* in which they were entered. In New Zealand it took a Maori chieftain three days to recite, before a government land commission, the descent of his people for thirty-four generations in order to justify their claim to certain territory. From generation to generation he gave the names, not only in the direct male line, but in the agnate branches stemming from each generation. Many Welsh pedigrees, traced back to the early kings of both North and South Wales, were handed on by trained bards for many generations before they were finally written down. Historical scholarship has found the documentary proof which substantiates the authenticity and accuracy of many of those ancient pedigrees, so their reliability should not be too hastily denied.

To my knowledge, which is limited because my experience has been gained chiefly from studying the families and records of New England, and their migrations westward across New York State into the Middle West, there is at least one black family in the United States whose history has been faithfully and accurately memorized and handed on from generation to generation, beginning with the progenitor who was brought from Africa on a slave ship in the eighteenth century. Probably there are many others.

The story of this one family has been so poignantly told by one of the descendants, Alex Haley, that I cannot refrain from abridging and paraphrasing it as an example of what may be done to verify a family tradition such as his. As a boy in western Tennessee, he squatted beside his grandmother's chair and listened while she and her visiting sisters and cousins talked about their forefathers, and their traditional lineage, which made a deep impression on him.

In maturity, Mr. Haley remembered that his grandmother always referred to her progenitor as "the African" who came to "Naplis," whom she sometimes called Kintay, and that she said he was cutting down a tree to make a drum when he was captured. Also, she used words which were strange to the boy, often enough to impress them upon his memory, words like *ko* for a banjo, and *Kamby Bolong*, which meant a large river, and others, some of which she repeated to herself while working about the house. She talked also about the successive generations from the African, using the names of each individual, what he did, and where he lived. Then, one day in 1965, when he was walking by the National Archives in Washington, he suddenly remembered his grandmother's account of the family history, so, upon impulse, he went in and asked if there were census records of Alamance County, N.C., where her people had lived about 1860–70. In these records he found the first confirmation of the accuracy of his grandmother's recollections: her grandfather and his family were listed! Another step was to identify the language or dialect to which those strange words that she used belonged. At the University of Wisconsin he found Dr. Vansina, an African professor of linguistics, who, listening intently to Mr. Haley's repetition of them, told him that the dialect was known as Mandinka in which the word for river was *Bolong*, which, combined with *Kamby*, undoubtedly referred to the Gambia River in West Africa. With this knowledge, Mr. Haley went to Bathurst, at the mouth of the Gambia, where he learned the location of the tribe which spoke that dialect but he had to return to America before he could organize a safari. Finally, months later, the officials in Bathurst wrote him that they had learned that a *griot* (very old man) who could recite the history of the Kinte tribe was living at Juffure, miles away up the river in the interior and invited him to return to Africa, which he did. From the *griot* he heard the history of the Kinte tribe and was told that a young man of the village, named Kinte, went into the forest one day to cut a tree and make a drum—the very tradition which Mr. Haley had heard his grandmother repeat. Kinte was captured and was never seen again. The *griot* also told him about the tribe from the time it left Old Mali and migrated to Mauretania, whence, later, Kairaba Kunta Kinte, a Moslem Marabout (holy man), came into Gambia and settled in Juffure. This man was the grandfather of Kinte, "the African" who came to 'Naplis (Annapolis, Md.) in 1767.

Those who wish to read the full story, which I have so briefly outlined, may look up Mr. Haley's article in the *New York Times Magazine*, July 16, 1972. He is expanding this article into a book, to be called *Roots*, which Doubleday will publish. I am confident it will be good reading and worth the time of any genealogist. Mr. Haley is collecting books and manuscripts for a library of black genealogy consisting of source materials such as plantation records, announcements of auction sales of slaves, bills of sale, and anything else that identifies black families. He urges, as I do, people (especially older members of families) to put on record, either on paper or on tape, their recollections of their family life and migrations. Such material may be sent to him at the Kinte Foundation, National Press Building, Washington, D.C. 20004.

Although not all who wish to trace black ancestry may have such success, I believe that anyone who reads this book may learn from Mr. Haley's experience what steps to take. Obviously, as I have said in Chapter Two, the first step is to glean all you can from your older relatives, noting carefully names and places as well as incidents which seem to be true, and then verify them, as both Mr. Perin and Mr. Haley have done, in order to discover the real history of the family.

CHAPTER FOUR

Out of the Family Papers

WHILE YOU are talking with Grandfather and the other older relatives try to find out if they have any written records of the family. Sometimes, as I have said, this requires tact, for the owners may be perversely inclined to think that you want to run off with some document; at other times, you can ask outright to see the family Bible and other papers and easily obtain permission to make a copy of the records which they contain, so you have to play it by ear. If Grandfather happens to be in the right mood, he may even give you the Bible, but beware lest by accepting it you are going to offend Aunt Mamie. A timely refusal may win her eternal good will and perhaps, later, even the Bible itself.

If you are at a distance from these older relatives and have to seek by correspondence any records which they may have, be sure to tell them that you are compiling a history of the family (promise them a copy, if need be), for sometimes they may suspect, however far it may be from the truth, that you are getting ready to claim some mythical "estate." It is truly amazing how many people have a notion that their family is entitled to some great estate in England. They have heard of the "Drake estate," or the "Buchanan estate," or the "Edwards estate"; or they have read in the newspapers about the litigation over the Wendell estate, and seen printed lists of the great number of claimants. Colonel Green, the famous Hetty's son, hadn't been dead a month when three women came into the genealogical library in the city where I live, to attempt to find records proving that they were among the rightful heirs to the Green and Howland millions. The old estates, so frequently dangled before the eyes of the susceptible, have long since been outlawed; those recently in the courts are of such a nature that very explicit proof must be established by any claimant. So be careful to avoid suspicion that you are going to steal evidence which will enable you to claim property.

Sometimes old letters, diaries, and other family papers exist. One or two old letters, in faded handwriting, badly worn along the creases, may contain clues to places of residence or details of family history which would otherwise be completely lost in the obscurity of the past. Sometimes a dull old diary will contain, interspersed among accounts of the weather, notes of baptisms, weddings, and funerals. Old family account books are another source of information, perhaps meager, but sometimes very illuminating. Even the framed sampler, worked by Great-Great-Aunt Hannah at the age of eleven, may prove to be of value. Don't overlook such items, for everything is grist to the genealogist's mill.

Let us take a look first at the family Bible. If other evidence is lacking, Bible records are accepted as reliable by practically all the hereditary and patriotic societies, such as the Society of Colonial Wars, the Colonial Dames, the Daughters of the American Revolution, and the Sons of the American Revolution. But the genealogist should use them with care. Occasionally someone has tampered with a Bible record, attempted to change a date or erase an entry altogether, although generally any alteration that has been made can be easily and quickly detected. An instance of such tampering comes to my mind. I was gathering data for a history of the family and wanted the record of the immediate family of a double cousin of mine, a woman of my grandfather's age (he was then in his eighties). She was inclined to be a bit vain and couldn't "remember" her own age! So I finally persuaded her to let me see her husband's family Bible—it was my second or third visit. When I came to the entry of her birth (her husband's father had meticulously entered the birth dates of the husbands and wives of his several children), I found that the year had been scratched out, although the month and day were there. Now it happens that I always carry a magnifying glass in my pocket for use in deciphering old handwriting and faded records. So, with a pretense of being unable to read some of the writing, which really was faded, I looked at the date which she thought she had eradicated and, catching a faint residue of the ink, was able to make out "1831." Later, I verified this through my grandfather (she was his first cousin), who remembered that she was just about two years younger than he was. Really, there is little that can be done to a written record which cannot be detected upon careful examination.

The genealogist may puzzle for hours and perhaps worry for months over certain problems connected with the use of Bible records. Some such records are remarkably full; others, unusually scant and inadequate. In one old Bible with which I am familiar (the volume was printed in 1609), the records begin about 1650 and give the name, the exact hour and minute of birth, and the sign of the zodiac under which each child was born (in those days astrology and the casting of horoscopes were taken seriously, so it was considered important to know these details). I have seen some eighteenth- and early nineteenth-century Bibles containing this same sort of meticulous record. Other Bibles have such exasperatingly meager data as "My wife was delivered of a son at six o'clock p.m. November the 12th, 1785"—with no name given.

Often one comes across a Bible with a record beginning like this:

Grandfather David Richardson, born 1700, died August 1770
Remember Richardson, born 1703, died August 1760

followed by a list of their children, with dates of birth and death given. Such a record is obviously not a contemporary record, and was made many, many years after "Grandfather" was born, for David Richardson would never have called himself "grandfather." On the face of it, it looks as though David Richardson had married Remember Richardson (indeed, the present owner of this very Bible had interpreted the record in that way);

but one should be suspicious of such a record, for, although occasionally cousins of the same surname did marry, it was not a very common practice. Further search in this particular case disclosed the fact that David Richardson's wife was Remember Ward. The granddaughter who made this record knew her only as Remember Richardson and therefore entered that name in the Bible.

Very few Bibles contain records dated before the eighteenth century, and most of the many which I have examined commence with records dated in the 1780's and 1790's. Most of the older Bibles have disappeared, although once in a while they do turn up in unexpected places. For example, the Greene family Bible, containing records dating from early in the seventeenth century, turned up in the possession of a descendant of an entirely different surname out in Nebraska, sixteen hundred miles away from Rhode Island, where the first record was entered in it. So, however remote the possibility, don't entirely give up hope of finding one for which you are looking, perhaps in the possession of a third or fourth cousin, or even in a bookshop

One of the first things to do when examining a Bible is to determine when the book was printed. If the title page has the date 1817 on it, or the preface or translator's note is signed 1817, you know at once that any records dated before that year were entered from memory (or, perhaps, copied from some older Bible). In this event these records should be carefully verified, if possible, from other sources—gravestones, town or church records. Records of births, marriages, and deaths occurring after that date were probably entered soon after they occurred. If, on the other hand, the Bible was published in 1609, and that printed date is found on its title page or on the half titles which mark the beginnings of the Old and New Testaments, and if the *handwriting in which the records were written* is of several different periods, then you may be reasonably certain that you have a genuine old record, containing, perhaps, several generations of the family births, marriages, and deaths.

Occasionally a son was sufficiently interested in his family, when he was married and was about to start his own family life, to copy from the original Bible, kept by his father, the data which it contained. But this rarely happened, for, I regret to say, our ancestors were not always of a genealogical turn of mind, and generally did not think of doing such a thing. Young people are always more interested in the future, as they should be, than in the past, however much they can learn from it.

Generally speaking, late in the eighteenth century and early in the nineteenth, a young couple, newly married and just starting out in life, either received a brand-new Bible as a gift from parents or well-wishers, or bought one with their first spare cash. It was a period during which "respectable people" still belonged to a church and read the Bible regularly. Sometimes they would enter their family names, but more frequently they were content to enter only the dates of their own births, that of their marriage, and then, from time to time as the children came along, the records of their progeny. Fortunately, in many nineteenth-century Bibles parents entered the name of the place as well as the date of birth. This was a century of great movement, as families by the thousands were migrating westward, staying but a few years in one place and then moving on as they heard of richer lands.

Not infrequently there is a question about the authenticity of the dates of the records in the family Bible. If the handwriting in which the records are made gives evidence of contemporary entry, there can be little question, however. You all know that your handwriting has varied from year to year as you have grown older. Just compare your diary of ten years ago with that written last month, if you want an example. So, if the handwriting of these old records varies from entry to entry, if the ink seems to be of a different quality in each of them, you may be certain that the data were entered as each child came along. But if there is a "copperplate" evenness about the handwriting, then, if the records do not tally with others which you have found, you will have to prove the correctness of one record or the other. For instance, there may be a difference between the record of your grandmother's birth as it is given in the Bible and that which you have found in the official records of the town in which she was born. Perhaps the baptismal record on the church books may settle the question, if it is the matter of the correct year, and sometimes the gravestone will determine it, although gravestone inscriptions are quite likely to have been made from Bible records. Sometimes it is impossible to settle the question. In that event you should carefully give both of the dates you have found, one in parentheses following the other, indicating, of course, which is which, thus:

> Sarah Richardson, born in Newton, Mass., 14 April 1774 (Newton records; her Bible record gives the date 1773); died 23 January 1848, "aged 74" (according to an obituary notice).

Generally, in the case of such a discrepancy, the town records should be accepted as more reliable. In this particular case, Sarah (Richardson) Clough wrote up her Bible record when she was well along in years and may have made an error of a year in her age (although people are generally given credit for knowing their own age). If she was born in 1773, as her Bible states, she would not have been seventy-five until three months after her death, and therefore the newspaper obituary was correct in stating that she was "aged 74" at the time of her death. But sometimes, when the birthday is approaching, the age on that birthday is given in such a notice, and even on the gravestone. Generally, I have noted that, in such a case, the person concerned was within a few weeks of the birthday—not as many as three months. The genealogist, however, to protect himself against the accusation of inaccuracy, should always note such a discrepancy, give both of the dates he has found, and perhaps also explain his reason for accepting either one or the other.

Sometimes a Bible record has been commenced by a young married couple in this way:

> Luther Whitney, born 23 February 1781
> Hannah Whitney, born 27 December 1777

This type of record, unlike the one of identical surnames in the Richardson family Bible, quoted above, offers no hint that Whitney may not have been actually the maiden name of the wife. Ostensibly Luther Whitney married Hannah Whitney (the date and place of the marriage were not entered in the Bible), but I am always skeptical when I come across such a Bible record, especially when no other record verifies the wife's name. I feel reasonably certain, in this case, that Hannah's maiden name was not Whitney because it has been impossible to establish her in any of the Whitney families in or around Adams, Mass., where their first two children were born. It is, of course, possible that she was a cousin, or belonged to some other Whitney family; the name is not uncommon.

If you cannot get possession of the Bible record which is important to you, get either a certified copy, sworn to before a notary public, or a photocopy or photostat of the record for your notebook. Moreover, if you cannot have the Bible to keep, it is always wise to make a careful note of the full name and address of the person who owns the Bible and the date on which you made the copy. Then, if you ever need to use that record for legal purposes or as a basis for membership in one of the hereditary or patriotic societies, you have certified evidence of this link in your ancestry, for you can submit your copy of this record to the society, with the name and address of its owner, and their genealogist can probably gain access to it for verification if desired.

Another sort of family record unfortunately much less common in occurrence than a Bible, but very valuable when it is found, is an old diary. Some diaries are exceedingly interesting, not only because they contain a wealth of genealogical details, but also because they were written by keen observers and display considerable evidence of the writer's personality. Unfortunately, sometimes the keeper of the diary was more interested in the affairs which were going on about him than he was in the details for which the genealogist is looking. In that case, however interesting they may be, the diaries are a disappointment; they should be carefully read, nevertheless, for there may be some important clues buried in them.

One mid-nineteenth-century diary, which I happen to

know, is almost purely a business record. The author was a miller in a small town, so he recorded each day just how many bushels of corn, wheat, and oats he ground in his mill, and how many feet of lumber were sawed. But he generally noted also the name of the individual for whom he ground or sawed. This has made the diary valuable to me in helping others trace their ancestry, and has enabled me to determine when some of the houses in town were built. But this diarist recorded also just which members of his family went to church each Sunday, so, in the absence of other records, we have been able to determine just when his sons and daughters broke away from under the rooftree. When he mentioned a funeral he was exasperatingly brief and made such statements as "Went to Florence's funeral." No clue to Florence's identity. One entry puzzled me a long time: "Went to Aunt Debbie's funeral." I knew of no Aunt Debbie or Deborah in the family. She proved to be a local character of such kindliness that she was "aunt" to everyone who knew her. Another exasperating entry was "Thomas came from the West for a visit" and a month later, "Thomas started back West." Finally I learned that this Thomas was his cousin, the only son of his only uncle, who had moved west to Illinois. That is the last record I have been able to find about Thomas, for this branch of the family appears never to have heard of him again.

Tantalizing as such diaries are, they must be carefully studied, for the alert mind will find much of use in them. It is a good plan to make careful notes of any names mentioned in them, for sometimes such names may prove to be of importance to you. In this same diary I noted that the diarist went to "Thomas Morse's funeral" on a given date. This entry, although it was of no immediate use to me, since I was then tracing my own ancestry, later enabled me to help a correspondent who was searching for the date of the death of her great-grandfather in order to complete her papers for the Daughters of the American Revolution. The town records did not contain the required information, and it was not until some time later that we found his gravestone in a forgotten cemetery.

While we are on the subject of diaries, there are many
invaluable colonial diaries which have been found and
printed. These very old diaries frequently enable a genealogist to prove a line of descent, and sometimes they
make very good reading, furnishing a picture of the times
in which their authors lived. Samuel Sewell's *Diary* (published by the Massachusetts Historical Society) is one of
the most important documents that we have, for he loved
functions and attended every christening, wedding, and
burial that came to his notice. He tells also just what
dowry he had to give each of his several wives. It is
amusing to note that they came cheaper as he and the
prospective spouse got older (perhaps the ladies had less
chance of getting a husband as their ages increased).
The judge, for he was a judge and even sat on the
famous witchcraft trials, lived in Boston, so his diary was
concerned with that vicinity. He kept a diary during the
latter half of his life, which covered the period from
1674 to 1729. An even older diary, the years including
from 1653 to 1684, is that of Thomas Minor, born in
England, who became one of the first settlers of Stoning-
ton, Conn. It is replete with information regarding those
who lived there during the pioneer days of the settlement, and was published in 1899 by one of his descendants. Joshua Hempstead's diary, covering thirty-seven
years between 1711 and 1748, does much the same thing
for New London, Conn. John Winthrop's *Journal*, which
has never been published in its entirety, is another invaluable source for Massachusetts and Connecticut families. He was a physician of a sort and made detailed
records of many of his cases.

Family letters are likewise worth reading. Not unlike
diaries, they frequently present a wealth of detail, although surnames are seldom mentioned in them, and
they may shed considerable light on the character and
personality of the writer. The one surviving letter written
by my great-great-grandmother gives us a vivid picture
of her personality and amplifies and confirms the family
tradition concerning her characteristics in pecuniary matters. This particular letter was written to her son in
Michigan about a month after her mother's death in
1839. She baldly states the fact that "Mother has been

dead nearly a month and I haven't gotten my share of her things yet!" Even without the tradition that she quarreled with her husband because he loaned some of her money without her consent, and that she refused to speak to him again until it was repaid (about seven years later), we get from this single sentence in her letter an unforgettable picture of the redoubtable old lady and her determination that no one should do her out of her rights.

Another old letter among the family papers set me on the right road to determining the descendants of a different branch of the family. This was written in a fine schoolgirlish hand on dainty paper such as, about a hundred years ago, could be found only in cities. In it were mentioned all such parties and visits as a young girl loves, and a number of names of cousins of whose existence I had been unaware. Another such letter, written in the 1840's and full of news about widely scattered relatives, enabled its finder to trace her family back several generations because it gave her the necessary clues to the places where they had lived.

Family account books also help considerably. Once, while attending a country auction in a Vermont hamlet, I pulled out of a basket of trash which was set aside to be burned (not even put up at auction) a long, narrow daybook. The entries dated from about 1803 to 1825 and contained many names of individuals and places. Through it I was able to establish the locality from which this family had come to Vermont and the date at which the migration was made. Aside from such details, of importance in a family history, this old account book sheds light on the prices of labor and materials prevailing at that time, especially in a rural community.

An account book, or ledger, in the possession of a gentleman in New York, proves to be practically a census of a small community in Dutchess County, for it was kept by a storekeeper. It contains evidence of the approximate dates of marriages, deaths, and removals, as the accounts are opened and closed or as the names of the customers are changed. From it I was able to prove almost to a month the date of the migration of my own family from that Dutchess County village to northern

Vermont, for I noted the date on which the account was closed and marked "Paid in full." By comparing that date with those of some deeds in Vermont, I could set the date of migration. R. E. Dale, of Lincoln, Neb., edited this old account book of Dunkin's Store, Dover Furnace (Pawling Precinct), N.Y., and published it in the genealogical department of the *Boston Evening Transcript,* June 28, July 10, and July 18, 1935, as note 2751.

Although you may never have examined very closely the sampler hanging in its frame on the wall it may contain data for your history. Sometimes a little seamstress, doing her cross-stitching, worked into the sampler a list of her brothers and sisters and their ages. If she dated the sampler (as many samplers are dated), you know approximately when each of the relatives was born. Sometime, if you are interested, get Edith Standwood Bolton's *American Samplers* from the library and examine it. Not only a fascinating account, it is a genealogical source book as well, for Mrs. Bolton has illustrated a number of samplers and given the family data from many more.

Another type of needlework which is of value to the ancestor hunter is the so-called "friendship" quilt and its variations. About a hundred and fifty years ago it was the vogue to work quilts made up of pieces on which were embroidered or signed in indelible ink the names of the maker's close friends and relatives. Sometimes the girls who inscribed their names even embroidered the pieces themselves and presented them to the maker, who put them together. One quilt of this kind, in the possession of a descendant of the Standish family, contains the names and dates of all the members of the family, including aunts and cousins. On it was based a claim to membership in the Daughters of the American Revolution, and membership in the Society of Mayflower Descendants might be established through the evidence it contains. This particular quilt has been written up in the *Daughters of the American Revolution Magazine* (Vol. 63, April 1929, pp. 219–24); a photograph of it is reproduced as an illustration to the article.

Another coverlet enabled one ancestor hunter to trace her family back across half a dozen states to the locality from which her ancestors came. It was embroidered by a great-grandmother for her hope chest. Taking a justifiable pride in her craftsmanship, she worked into one panel of the "spread" her maiden name, the date, and the name of the town in Maine in which she was then living.

Even old family silver may prove useful to the genealogist. Although very old silver is uncommon, an occasional piece has survived and been preserved as an heirloom. An old spoon engraved thus:

A B
C

has its clue, for initials placed in this manner on really old silver generally mean that that piece belonged to a husband and wife jointly. In this case, let us say Abijah and Betsy Cole. It may have been a wedding gift. Old tankards and silver mugs are frequently engraved in the same manner. Sometimes it is difficult to identify such initials, but they do serve as a clue which may put you on the right track. Recently, reading the will of Captain Lawrence Clarke, of Newport and Middletown, R.I., instead of depending upon the published abstract of it, I noted that he bequeathed to his son Lawrence "the silver cup marked L T which belonged to my grandfather." Captain Clarke's mother's maiden name had not been known hitherto; his own given name is not found in any of the earlier generations of his father's family. There was a Lawrence Turner living in Newport in the seventeenth century, but, as far as the town records show, no other man with the initials L T. Was Margaret, the second wife of the Reverend Joseph Clarke, the daughter of Lawrence Turner? We think so. One other slight bit of circumstantial evidence seems to confirm this assumption: Lawrence Turner was called a brick maker in one document; Lawrence Clarke, when he was not much over sixteen, was granted permission by the town council to dig clay for bricks. This indicates that he may have been apprenticed to his grandfather, whose silver cup he later possessed.

Thus you see an important adjunct to the family

memories is any record which may exist in the family archives or possession. You should always try to locate such records, and with their aid get the older relatives to explain as much about the family as possible. Sometimes the sight of an old letter or a bit of silver recalls to an aging mind the story back of it or relationships which have been forgotten and might not otherwise come to mind. In digging for ancestors no stone is too small or too insignificant to be left unturned.

CHAPTER FIVE

Digging in Books and Libraries

BY THE time you have talked to or had correspondence
with the older relatives and perhaps the older friends of
the family, and have dug what you can out of the old
family papers and records, you will probably have gathered sufficient data in your notebook and on your chart
to begin searching in printed material. Perhaps you are
lucky enough to live near a library containing a genealogical collection, say in Boston, New York, Washington,
Chicago, Seattle, San Francisco, or Los Angeles, to mention only a few of the larger cities in which there are
well-known genealogical collections. This material may
be found in public libraries or other libraries, such as the
New England Historic Genealogical Society Library in
Boston, the Newbury Library in Chicago, the great collection of the Genealogical Society in Salt Lake City,
Utah, or the Library of Congress in Washington. Even
though your public library may not contain a special
collection of genealogical material, the librarian should
know where such collections can be found.

If you do not live near a genealogical library, large or
small, perhaps you can plan your vacation to include a
visit to a city in which there is a good collection. One of
my friends, whose family likes an annual trip to some
city, always manages to go to a place like Chicago, San
Francisco, or New York for his vacation. While his family enjoys the shops and city sights during the day, he,
with his notebook and the problems on which he is working, spends the time in the library, digging for his ancestors. Each year he comes back with a problem or two

solved and a sheaf of notes which keep him busy through
many of the long winter evenings.

If you have never used a genealogical collection before, the first thing to do is to have a good talk with the
curator or assistant in charge who, from long experience
in serving genealogists, knows how to help a beginner to
get started right. He knows also the collection under his
care and can efficiently direct your use of it. He will
explain its arrangement to you, and show you any special
indexes that have been made for it.

Once you have explained your problem to him, he will
get out for you any printed genealogies of the family or
families in which you are interested that are available
in this collection. You may be fortunate enough to have
such a genealogy put into your hands immediately and
to find in it your line of descent—once you have become
familiar with the system on which it is arranged. (A certain amount of study is required in order to pick up any
genealogy and use it intelligently, for the system of
arrangement varies a great deal from one volume to another.) In the event that you have such good fortune,
you can either copy the complete line of your descent
from the book before you or you can plan to buy a copy
of it from one of the booksellers who handle genealogical
books, such as Goodspeed's Book Shop in Boston, the
Genealogical Book Co. in Baltimore, Md., or the Chas.
R. Tuttle Co., Rutland, Vt. Sometimes the volume is rare,
for genealogies are almost always printed in small editions; hence a copy may be very difficult to find and very
expensive when found. But even if you are fortunate
enough to be able to afford to buy a copy you will want
to make a working pedigree from the copy in the library
as a basis for running back the female lines. No one
printed volume will be likely to contain all your ancestry; otherwise you would know about it and probably
not be reading this book.

Such a working pedigree looks something like the illustration on page 50. You will note that I have given, at
the top of the column at the left-hand side of the page,
the exact title of the volume used, and in that column,
opposite each generation, the references to the pages on
which the data for each generation were found. It is

THE DOANE FAMILY by A.A. DOANE

pp. 1-18   DEAC. JOHN DOANE =
Plymouth, ca. 1630
Died Eastham 21 Feb.
1685, ae. 95 yrs.

30 April 1662

pp. 21-26   JOHN DOANE, JR. = HANNAH BANGS, dau.
Born Plymouth | of Edward Bangs
ca. 1635; died | born ca. 1644, liv. 1677
Eastham 15 Mar. 1708
ae. 73 yrs.

3 Dec. 1696

p. 45   SAMUEL DOANE = MARTHA³ HAMBLEN
Born Eastham 2 Mar. 1673 | dau. of John² (James¹) and Sarah
Died Eastham 15 Aug. 1756 | (Bearse) Hamblen. Born Barnstable
3 Dec. 1696, living in 1734

1 Oct. 1730

p. 68   SIMEON DOANE = APPHIA HIGGINS
Born Eastham 1 Dec. 1708
Died Eastham 4 Dec. 1789

pp. 98-99   BENJAMIN DOANE = RUTH
Died North Brookfield, Mass. | Died at Eastham
Born Eastham, ca. 1738 | 16 Aug. 1778 ae. 39
3 Jan. 1824, ae. 86 yrs.

pp. 165-166   BENJAMIN DOANE = AZUBAH DOANE
Born Eastham 29 Aug. 1772 | Born 27 Sept. 1772
Died Bakersfield, Vt. | Died Bakersfield 27 June 1845
27 Aug. 1846 | (Her ancestry not given
| in Doane genealogy)

1 Dec. 1829

p. 298   JAMES HARVEY DOANE = PERSIS HOWE
Born Bakersfield, 20 Sept. 1802 | Born 4 Nov. 1807
Died Bakersfield, 18 June 1847 | Died 30 Sept. 1873

15 Feb. 1870

p. 298   BRADLEY JOHN DOANE = ELLEN H. RANDALL
Born Bakersfield, 9 Aug. 1846
Died Bakersfield, 22 June 1901

p. 298   HARRY HARVEY DOANE
Born Bakersfield 1 July 1873

FORM 3. The Doane Pedigree.

essential that you take such references as you go along. Otherwise you will have to check back through the volume to get them and use more valuable time later. Many a genealogist who started out without these references has cursed himself for the oversight when he has wanted them, especially if the book is in a distant library.

This pedigree is based on what I happened to find in first consulting the book entitled *The Doane Family,* by Alfred Adler Doane (Boston, 1902), in the New York State Library in Albany many years ago. Harry Harvey Doane, listed on page 298 of this book, was my father, so here I found my complete Doane line back to the immigrant, John Doane (or Done, as the name was then spelled), who appeared in Plymouth, Mass., about 1630. As you will note on this working pedigree, when I found this line I discovered my descent from the Bangs, Hamblen, Bearse, Higgins, Howe, and Randall families as well, and so I began to dig for the ancestors in those lines and work those pedigrees back to the immigrants, and, in one or two cases, across the Atlantic into England, and for two or three generations there. I found printed genealogies for the Hamblen (that is, Hamlin) and Higgins families but I have had to do a lot of digging for the rest. I have not yet found Azubah Doane, my great-great-grandmother!

Now, even though you find such a line in print, you must be very careful about accepting it as correct in every detail. Not everything that glitters is gold, and not everything that is printed is true, in spite of the popular belief. Genealogies are compiled and published, sometimes at great expense, by all sorts of people. Some of these records are reliable and trustworthy; some of them are filled with glaring errors. A beautifully printed genealogy, elaborately bound in tooled leather, may be full of mistakes and almost worthless, or even worse than that, grossly misleading. Another family history, printed on cheap paper from worn type, may prove to be notable for its accuracy. You cannot tell from the outward appearance and the physical make-up, although as a general rule a book breeds confidence if it is carefully printed on good paper and substantially and tastefully bound in cloth. By studying the contents of a volume you can form a pretty good idea of the intelligence, acumen, and accuracy of the author or compiler.

If there are discrepancies in dates, for instance, you should be suspicious and check carefully. Suppose that you find that John Jones, who emigrated to America in 1630 and died in Dorchester, Mass., in 1685, aged eighty years, is stated, in the book before you, to have been the son of Sir William Jones, of Buxton, Herts, England. In reading the chapter on the English origin of the family, you note that Sir William, reputed father of John, the emigrant, died in 1600 and was buried at Buxton. If you stop to figure John's possible birth date, you will see that there is obviously something wrong, for no man who died in 1600 could be the father of a child born in 1605. This sounds ridiculous, doesn't it? Yet, I have known unheeding ancestor hunters to accept such a statement "because they found it in print." Obviously, anyone who would allow such an error to be printed is careless; therefore anything you find in a genealogy compiled by such an author should be carefully checked—by the original records, if possible.

Sometimes the genealogist or compiler of the book does not actually make such a statement, but the person using it makes a careless assumption from the documents which the compiler has printed in his genealogy. For instance, many of the descendants of Deacon John Doane of Plymouth and Eastham, Mass., who have used A. A. Doane's book have assumed that the Deacon's wife was named Abigail. This assumption is based on the will which Mr. Doane copied from the Registry of Probate at Barnstable, Mass. John Doane, in his will, dated in 1678 (misprinted 1768 in the book), bequeathed his dwelling house and a certain "upland and meadow" about it to his "loving wife." Since Abigail Doane certified to the truthfulness of the inventory of his estate in 1686, it has been assumed that she was his widow and the mother of his children. Now Mr. Doane also printed a verbatim copy of a deed, dated in 1681, in which John Doane conveyed this same dwelling house and "upland and meadow" about it to his daughter Abigail. Obviously his wife had died between 18 May 1678, the date of his will, and 2 December 1681, the date of this deed. Hence, the Abigail

Doane who certified the inventory must have been his daughter, to whom he had deeded the house originally intended for his widow if she survived him. Later research by another genealogist indicates that Deacon John Doane had a wife named Ann in 1648 when they both signed a conveyance, who was dead before 1659 when he and his wife Lydia conveyed some land in Eastham (see Mary Walton Ferris's *The Dawes-Gates Ancestral Lines,* Chicago, 1931, 1943, Vol. 2, pp. 304-5).

I doubt if there is a genealogy that does not contain a typographical error or misprint, and there are very few in which there are not some mistakes made by the compiler in interpreting the records at his disposal. You should be alert to catch these, and, whenever you see one, try to check it against the original records. Not infrequently you may find that a genealogist has killed off the child from whom you know you are descended, because he did not find that child mentioned in its father's will, or for some other such reason. In a case of this kind you must be careful to supply ample proof of your ancestor's life and connection with the parents.

Failing a published genealogy of the family in which you are interested, the curator of the collection in which you are working will show you how to find any genealogies of the family that have been printed in periodicals as well as genealogies of other families with which yours is connected, and local histories. Or he will show you how to get at these "buried" genealogies through such indexes as Jacobus's, Durrie's, and Munsell's (for a list of such indexes see Appendix A). These indexes vary in completeness. Some are limited but thorough in covering the ground which they are supposed to cover. (Always read the preface and see what the compiler's intentions were.) Others, although they are supposed to be adequate, are very much out of date. Some libraries have compiled indexes to their genealogical collections. For example, the Newberry Library, Chicago, indexed family sketches in all local histories it acquired until about 1917. This index has been reproduced by offset printing and is available in several of the large libraries. *The American Genealogical Index,* conceived by Fremont J. Rider, of Middletown, Conn., is another valuable tool, for it combines in one alphabetical order all the names in a considerable number of genealogies, thus making it short work to locate a given name (watch, however, for variant spellings). A second series, *The American Genealogical-Biographical Index,* is in course of publication; it includes all names in the Genealogical Department of the *Boston Evening Transcript,* 1906–41 (see page 59), the many lists of Revolutionary War soldiers, and several more genealogies.

Frequently such an index will be very useful to you. Although the library in which you are working may not have the volumes to which it refers, if you can get the names of the authors and the titles of such books, you can make a note to use them in some other library where they are to be found, or perhaps, ask some friend to consult them for you.

If you do not find a reference to the family in which you are interested, the next thing to do is to locate a history of the town or country in which you know they lived. Even though your family may have been too obscure to warrant a genealogy of it in the history of that town, you may find a valuable clue there. For instance, by studying the history of the town of Fairfield in Abby Maria Hemenway's *Vermont Historical Gazetteer,* I found that many of the settlers of that town came from Connecticut, mainly from Litchfield and Fairfield counties, or from Dutchess County, N.Y., which borders Connecticut. I noted that many of the grantees of Fairfield, Vt., were from New Fairfield, Conn., and later discovered that New Fairfield was settled by families from around Fairfield, Conn. The very names of the towns are indicative of these facts. This led me, first, to Mrs. Elizabeth Hubbell Schenck's *History of Fairfield, Connecticut,* where I found the clues for my Gilbert line and those cognate to it; and later to Donald Lines Jacobus's *History and Genealogy of the Families of Old Fairfield,* where they were given more accurately and completely.

There is, unfortunately, no comprehensive and up-to-date bibliography of local history, although bibliographies of varying completeness exist for some of the states. The New York State Library has published bibliographies for Maine, Connecticut, and New York, which are now sadly out of date, but still very useful for material published years ago. Hammond has compiled a bibliography of local histories of New Hampshire towns. Flagg has done a similar piece of work for Massachusetts towns. There are now genealogical guides to many more states. Such bibliographies, when they exist, enable you to learn very quickly whether or not there are any printed records about the locality in which your family lived. Once you have the reference, you can generally obtain access to it and examine it or have it examined for you.

If your library has no such bibliography and is too small to have a genealogical collection, you should secure a copy of the *Catalogue of Genealogies and Local Histories,* which is issued at intervals of two or three years by Goodspeed's Book Shop, 18 Beacon Street, Boston, Mass. 02108. There is a small charge for handling and mailing. Although it lists only the books which Goodspeed has for sale, it is invaluable to the genealogist, for Goodspeed's stock is large and makes a specialty of genealogical books. Other bookshops deal in genealogies, and two, Chas. E. Tuttle, Rutland, Vt. 05701, and the Genealogical Book Co., Baltimore, Md. 21202, publish catalogues. These catalogues are almost the only inexpensive bibliographies of genealogies and local histories to be obtained.

You should become familiar, however, with two extensive printed lists of genealogies, which are arranged under family names. One of these is, to give it its exact title, the list of *American and English Genealogies in the Library of Congress,* which was published in Washington in 1919 and therefore contains only the genealogies that were in the National Library before August 1919. A new edition was published in 1972, but it is very expensive, although of great value. This list has cross references, so it frequently furnishes a clue to a "buried" genealogy. Another list is that published by the Long Island Historical Society, of Brooklyn, N.Y., in 1935. It is called *Catalogue of American Genealogies in the Library of the Long Island Historical Society;* it lists over eight thousand books dealing with genealogy, as well as about eight hundred and fifty manuscripts, typescripts, and photostat copies of original wills, etc. By looking up your family in either or both of these volumes, you can quickly determine whether or not a genealogy of interest to you has been published. You may find one and you may not. If you do, you may find in it what you want; or you may have considerable digging to do before you can connect your line with those given in it.

In addition to the printed genealogies and local histories, the curator of a genealogical collection will give you an introduction to the genealogical magazines covering the part or parts of the country in which you are interested. The oldest and most comprehensive periodical devoted to genealogy is the *New England Historical and Genealogical Register,* familiarly known as the *Register,* the first number of which was published in January 1847, under the aegis of the New England Historic Genealogical Society. Consolidated indexes to Vols. 1–50 and 51–112 have been published. The latter was privately printed; it is not a complete index of all names, but rather a subject index. Genealogies of a great many families have been published in it, so you should not allow the local nature of its title to keep you from looking through its indexes for any material for which you may be looking. Quite naturally the preponderance of the material is about New England families, but many of these families are now scattered throughout the United States. In addition to genealogies, this journal contains many transcripts and abstracts of local records, such as town records, probate records, church records, and copies of cemetery inscriptions from many New England towns. For years the society has maintained a Committee on English Research, and published the results of careful and painstaking research on the English origin of American families. Another committee of this society has been compiling a record of American families possessing authentic coats of arms. Eight parts of this roll have been published, carefully illustrated with drawings of the arms. The first two parts were published in the *Register,* Vol. 82 (April 1928), pp. 146–68, and Vol. 86 (July 1932), pp. 258–86, and later were issued as reprints. All parts have appeared in pamphlet form. The title page and index of all eight parts have been compiled and will

be published in 1973, so it will soon be possible to bind
them together in one volume. The committee has registered several hundred coats as authentic and rightfully
borne or used by their respective families. Undoubtedly
additional parts will be published as more coats of arms
are authenticated and the roll grows.

The *New York Genealogical and Biographical Record*
is another important periodical for the genealogist. As
the title indicates, this is devoted mainly to records pertaining to New York. In it have been published transcripts of the 1800 census for several of the counties in
that state, as well as genealogies, cemetery inscriptions,
abstracts of wills and deeds, and other valuable contributions. The *American Genealogist* (formerly the *New
Haven Genealogical Magazine*) is yet another excellent
periodical and is devoted exclusively to New England
records prior to 1800 and to studies of genealogical problems rather than long detailed genealogies. *Tyler's Genealogical Quarterly*, the *William and Mary Quarterly*, and
the *Virginia Magazine of Biography and History* are all
devoted mainly to Virginia genealogy. The *Pennsylvania
Magazine* contains a great deal of genealogy. The *National Genealogical Society Quarterly*, published in
Washington, D.C., has reprinted some of its more general articles in a series entitled "Special Publications"
which are very useful. There are many other genealogical magazines (most of them much younger than those
mentioned) which are devoted to the interests of special
parts of the country or to special fields of research. A
complete list of these would be too detailed for our purpose, but you can easily find their names if you begin
poking about in a library for them. There are over a hundred of them!

In addition to the magazines now being published,
there are many that were comparatively short-lived, but
that contain material of great importance to the ancestor
hunter. Such a magazine as the *Old Northwest Genealogical Quarterly*, which was published between 1898
and 1912, is very valuable, for it contains many records
of interest to those who trace their ancestry through the
region known as the Old Northwest, particularly the
Western Reserve in Ohio. The series of magazines edited

by the late Eben Putnam, of Salem, Mass., a capable genealogist, is another valuable lot. The *Newport Historical Magazine* (later called the *Rhode Island Historical Magazine*) is another, for it contains transcripts of many early records of that locality.

Most of these magazines, as well as several which are not mentioned here, have been indexed in Jacobus's *Index to Genealogical Periodicals*. It should be remembered that Mr. Jacobus indexed articles (that is, contributions pertaining to families) and local histories only and did not include in his index all the specific names of individuals mentioned in these periodicals. If he had included these, the cost of compiling and publishing such an index would have been prohibitive. Mr. Jacobus included in Vol. III (1953) his "Own Index" to genealogies which are "buried" in certain selected books containing ancestral lines and compiled by able genealogists. There is now an annual *Index to Genealogical Periodicals*, compiled and published by George Ely Russell, of Bowie, Md. He indexes about a hundred journals.

The late William Wade Hinshaw, of Washington, D.C., devoted the later part of his life to the publication of Quaker records. He compiled the first six large volumes of the *Encyclopedia of American Quaker Genealogy*. Vol. 1 covers the North Carolina meetings (remember that many New England Quakers moved to Pennsylvania and thence southward along the Appalachian valleys to North Carolina, then over the mountains and up through Tennessee and Kentucky to southern Ohio and Indiana); Vol. 2 includes four Philadelphia meetings; Vol. 3, New York City and Long Island meetings; Vols. 4 and 5, the Ohio meetings; and Vol. 6, the Virginia meetings. Vols. 7 and 8 contain the records of the Indiana meetings, compiled by Willard Heiss. Others may yet be published. These should never be overlooked, even though you may not be aware that once your family had Quaker affiliations. They may save you hours of searching, a long trip, and many dollars as well.

In all genealogical libraries worthy of the name you will find many other sources of genealogical material—manuscripts which have been deposited there, collections of clippings and other scattered material, and so forth.

One of the most important of these supplementary sources is the printed transcript of the 1790 census of the United States, taken in 1790 and 1791 and printed in 1909 by the Bureau of the Census. In a later chapter I shall have more to say about this valuable set of books and the census itself.

While we are discussing printed material mention must be made of the *Boston Evening Transcript* and its genealogical department. Back in 1876, at the suggestion of Oliver Wendell Holmes, the *Transcript* began a department of "Notes and Queries." By 1894 the genealogical queries had become so numerous that a separate department was devoted to them. As long as the *Transcript* was published (that is, until 1941) this department appeared, sometimes twice a week, at other times daily. A wealth of genealogical material was printed in this newspaper: queries from ancestor hunters, answers from others who had been successful in their quest; copies of gravestone inscriptions from forgotten and overgrown cemeteries (mainly in New England, to be sure), abstracts of probate records and deed books, carefully worked out genealogies, and so forth. Many notable genealogists contributed to the *Transcript* columns, and many arguments over disputed points were included. Much of the material was of a high standard of excellence, and, though some of it was pure guesswork and must be used with caution, it is worth looking at. Rider's *American Genealogical-Biographical Index*, as noted above (see page 53), is including all names which appeared in the *Transcript*'s columns between 1906 and 1941 (note that the earlier years are still unindexed). Since the pages containing the Genealogical Department have been reproduced on microcards and are usually available in the larger libraries having genealogical collections, this vast storehouse of data, much of it unavailable elsewhere, is now being opened for general use. You may find in it the very records for which you are searching.

The *Hartford Times* had a Genealogical Department in its Saturday issue for many years, beginning in 1933. Alas, this too has been given up.

Fortunately, in 1968 the Connecticut Society of Genealogists was organized and commenced the *Connecticut Nutmegger.* About half of this quarterly is given over to queries. Only members of the society may submit them, but each is allowed five in any one issue. Answers are not published and are mailed directly to the querist. Many members have reported excellent results, so membership seems worthwhile. Write to the Secretary, 16 Royal Oak Drive, West Hartford, Conn. 06107, for more information.

Another query medium of national scope was *Genealogy & History,* a magazine devoted entirely to queries and answers, which was published by Adrian Ely Mount.

The Everton Publishers, Logan, Utah, publish the *Genealogical Helper,* which has several special issues each year devoted to directories of libraries, genealogists, etc.

Libraries as a general rule will not lend genealogical books, either by mail or locally. They are too much in demand in the library. Moreover, most of them are extremely difficult to replace if they are inadvertently lost or destroyed or otherwise fail to get back to their home base. So do not ask if you may take them home, and do not request your local librarian to borrow them on interlibrary loan for your use.

The New England Historic Genealogical Society, however, does lend duplicates from its great collection of books to its members under certain conditions. If you want to do much digging at home, even though you may live a thousand miles or more away from "the home of the bean and the cod," it may be worth your while to apply for membership in that society. The address of the society is 101 Newbury Street, Boston, Mass. 02116, and the dues are fifteen dollars a year. Members receive the *New England Historical and Genealogical Register,* a quarterly of which I've already spoken, and may borrow duplicate books from the society's library.

While on the subject of societies, I should tell you that there are many of them. "N.E.," as many old hands call the one I've just mentioned, is the oldest and most distinguished. Many others are more or less active and flourishing, and a large number of them publish magazines of some sort. They range from purely local organizations which are, sometimes, nothing more than clubs, to state-wide groups which meet once a year. The *Genealogical Helper,* mentioned above, has a list of them. The American Association for State and Local History publishes a *Directory of Historical Societies and Agencies in the United States and Canada,* which is useful in locating local historical societies.

In using libraries, particularly by mail, you must remember that none has the staff to do extensive research for you, and most have a rule limiting the amount of time which may be spent in answering your questions. If it is obvious that much time will be required, you will probably be sent a list of local genealogists so you can make your arrangements directly with one of them. In considering their fees you must remember that you will be paying for experienced and even expert assistance which is more efficient than ordinary labor.

I shall not attempt to list all the genealogical libraries in the country because there is a special issue of the *Genealogical Helper* which lists them all every other year or so. This can be purchased for a small sum from the publishers in Logan, Utah.

CHAPTER SIX

Blowing the Dust Off the Town Records

WHEN YOU have tried to connect the lines that you have worked out from your family papers with those that you find in the books at the library, and perhaps have prodded the memories of your relatives a bit more in the process, you may find that you still lack a generation or two or must have more information before you can definitely establish your pedigree. Then you will want to get at the records of the town in which your people lived and find out what data can be had there. If you happen to live in the same community in which several generations of your family have lived, you will have many pleasant afternoons examining the records in the office of the town clerk or whatever the keeper of records happens to be called in your locality.

Take your chart and your notebook under your arm and make an expedition to that gentleman's office, use your most ingratiating manner (the one most suited to the person who has charge of the records), and ask him to let you see the records covering the period in which you are digging or, if he seems so inclined, actually to help you find the information that you want.

In recent years in some states laws have been enacted prohibiting unrestricted use of vital records by anyone other than genealogists or members of historical societies, so it is wise to find out what the law is before you ask for such records. Granted such laws may have been enacted to prevent scandalmongers from verifying (or using illegally) records of bastardy, bigamy, illegal marriages, etc., this precautionary measure works a hardship on those who have a valid right to see the records of their own people.

Even though in most states public records are public property, and you have a right to use them, some of the officials who keep those records may be very jealous of them and guard them from "alien hands." Others are more than helpful to those who are sufficiently interested in what they contain to take the time to study them and use them. Some town clerks are crotchety and cranky and grumble a lot about the trouble of getting down the big ledgers—I have rarely seen town records kept in a volume that is light of weight and easy to handle! Others appear to be annoyed, when they are really delightful old bears who grumble a bit merely to maintain their dignity but who really enjoy the diversion which you create by coming to them for information. Some insist upon a fee (the law in some states provides that a fee shall be paid for copies of old records); and others wave a hand and say "Come again!" It is up to you to size up the man (or, occasionally, the woman) and handle him with tact and consideration.

Sometimes such records are actually kept neatly in repair. Once I had occasion to stop in Belchertown, Mass., and look at the vital records of that town, which I found carefully preserved between layers of Japanese silk and in excellent condition. They were, as well, in the custody of a fine gentleman to whom it was a pleasure to talk. But more frequently the old ledgers are covered with dust and dog-eared, loose in their bindings and falling to pieces. Sometimes they have been thoroughly indexed, but more frequently there may be no index or, what is really worse, a poorly made, inaccurate, and inadequate one. Sometimes they have been carefully kept and are fairly complete, including much more than one would expect. I stopped one time in the town of Bridport, Vt., to get some records for a case on which I was working, and found a wonderful set of records which included not only the births, deaths, and marriages as they had been entered throughout the century and more of the town's existence, but also a complete transcript of all the cemetery inscriptions in town.

Only in rare instances are the early vital records of a

town kept in special volumes devoted exclusively to that purpose. Generally they are interspersed among other records, those of the business affairs and transactions of the town, land records, tax lists, and town accounts. The town clerk should know in which volumes there are to be found vital records, but many times it pays to go poking about yourself, if what he hands you does not contain the records for which you are searching—provided, of course, you have gained his confidence and thus secured his permission to enter the sanctum in which the records are kept. After you have been digging a very long time, you will have developed an instinct which seems to tele- graph from your subconscious mind the message: "That's the volume you want!" You begin to have hunches; and when you do, you should play them.

In many towns the records have actually been de- stroyed by fire—hard luck in such a case. In others they have been lost. Occasionally lost records are restored and sometimes records turn up after their existence had been completely forgotten. A few years ago in a certain town where I had done considerable searching, there was a change in the town clerkship, and the offices were cleaned up. I mean really cleaned, not merely swept. The great safe in which the volumes of town records were stored was actually moved out from the wall—for the first time in fifty years, probably. Behind it was found the thin, large, flat folio volume in which were the mid- nineteenth-century records of births, marriages, and deaths. It had slipped down there many years ago, and had never been missed. What problems it solved, and how eagerly I began to check carefully through it!

Although the date varies in the several states, there were practically no general laws requiring the registra- tion of births, marriages, and deaths before 1850; and in the states in which there were such laws they were fre- quently ignored or rather carelessly observed by the town officials. (In some cases they were ignored even after 1850 and up until the twentieth century.) So, you can never be sure that you will find the record for which you are searching.

However, we are going on the supposition that the records exist and that you have gained access to them.

Let us suppose that you have your chart complete through your Grandfather Merrick, that you have gone to the library and found a Merrick genealogy which does not "come down" to him, and that therefore you must work the line back another generation or two before you can make the "connection." Let us suppose that his name was Joseph Merrick and that you know he was born in Derby, N.H., about 1834. You have gone to the town clerk's office; he has put into your hands the volume covering that period. You begin to search for Merrick records. You find "Joseph, son of Jeremiah and Hannah Merrick, born 24 March 1833." Make a note of it and the page and number of the volume on which it was found— the date is near enough that of your Joseph to warrant an investigation of the record—and continue your search. Now, I'll grant you that your Joseph is the only one in which you are interested, but for the purposes of proof and identification the names of his brothers and sisters are useful and sometimes essential. So, if you are wise, you will take down the records of the other children of Jeremiah and Hannah Merrick, because someone may remember that Grandfather Merrick had a sister Hannah and a brother Jerry, or you may find a will at the probate court in which Jeremiah Merrick, Jr., directs that his property be divided between his brother Joseph and his sister Hannah, thus proving that your Joseph was identical with the son of Jeremiah and Hannah Merrick of that name.

But let us assume that in proceeding through the volume you find another Joseph Merrick, born there 2 June 1835, son of John and Mary Merrick; and perhaps even a third Joseph Merrick, son of Henry and Jane, born there 31 May 1834.

Now you have a problem. Which of these three Joseph Merricks was your grandfather? How are you going to prove one of them to be your grandfather? The name seems to be a common one in the Merrick family, and it is quite possible that all three Josephs were the grand-sons or great-grandsons of a progenitor named Joseph Merrick.

One method of identification is that of eliminating the Josephs who could not have been your grandfather.

Perhaps on further search you find that Joseph, son of
Henry and Jane Merrick, died in 1835. Thus one of them
is eliminated. And possibly, still further on, in another
volume of records, you find the marriage of Joseph Merrick and Sarah Jones on 25 December 1857. From your
family records you have already learned that your grandfather, Joseph Merrick, married Almira Buck, 30 June
1856. Obviously, this isn't the marriage record of your
grandfather, but you still don't know which Joseph Merrick was yours, especially since there was no indication
in this record of the parentage of the groom. You seem
to be up against a blank wall in your attempt to determine whether Jeremiah or John Merrick was your great-
grandfather.

The next thing to do is to take a look at the death record of your grandfather. As vital records came to be kept
systematically, and, especially, in the later part of the
nineteenth century when special ledgers were provided
for them, the parentage of the deceased was noted in his
death record (and in marriage records the parentage of
both the contracting parties). So, in looking at the official
town record of the death of your grandfather you may
find his parentage given.

But sometimes these details were overlooked by a
careless clerk or by the physician reporting the death.
Sometimes a man was so old that he was living with
grandchildren who did not know his parents' names and
the record was never turned in. For the sake of our
problem let us suppose that this was the case and the
death record of your Joseph Merrick gives no indication
of his parentage. Thus you are forced to continue your
search and must work your problem out by using other
records and even circumstantial evidence. That is why
I advised taking a complete list of the brothers and
sisters of each Joseph, as you came across them.

The easiest step to take next is to go to the probate
office, generally in the county seat, although occasionally
the probate district is not identical with the county and
the probate office is in another town.

But before you take that journey, look back still farther
in the vital records while you have access to them. Suppose that you find the marriage record of "Jeremiah

Merrick and Hannah Lyon, 21 May 1828." Suppose that your grandfather named his eldest daughter Hannah Lyon Merrick, and perhaps one of his sons James Lyon Merrick, possibly your father. Here is circumstantial evidence that your grandfather was connected with the Lyon family in some way—otherwise why his or his wife's insistence that the name "Lyon" be carried on by at least two of his children? It certainly looks reasonable that he named his eldest daughter after his mother, and perhaps his son after his grandfather Lyon—the case is even sounder if you find a record stating that James and Hannah Lyon had a daughter named Hannah, born, say, 21 August 1807 (thus old enough to be the Hannah Lyon who married Jeremiah Merrick in 1828).

Pending further proof from the probate records, or possibly the cemetery inscriptions, you may accept as probable this parentage of your grandfather, Joseph Merrick, and continue your search for another generation of the Merrick line, the parentage of Jeremiah Merrick, your hypothetical great-grandfather. If he married in 1828, he was probably at least twenty years old and therefore was born in 1808 or before, for few men married before they were twenty (it is more common to find a girl marrying before that age than it is to find a young man doing so). But your search through the earlier volumes of records does not produce the birth record of Jeremiah Merrick. Possibly he was born in another, perhaps a neighboring, town; or possibly his birth was not recorded. You should, however, make note of any other Merricks born during this period. Say you find a single Merrick record, that of the birth of a son to Joseph and Mary Merrick in 1805, no name given. This is tantalizing, for the unnamed son may have been your Jeremiah (or, of course, Henry or John). You find nothing more, on further search, not even the marriage of Joseph and Mary.

Now ask to see the land records, for they are very valuable to the genealogist. As we get farther back into the history of the country and vital records become more and more sketchy, these land records assume paramount importance. Even into the nineteenth century many land records are teeming with genealogical details. A husband

and wife may deed land jointly—in many states this was required if the land came into the family through the wife's inheritance. Sometimes a father would transfer land to his son "for love"; sometimes the heirs of an estate would give a joint deed, signed by all of them and even the wives and husbands of those who happened to be married—I have found one such deed which was signed by nineteen people, all of them descendants of the man who had owned that house and lot when he died; sometimes residence in other localities was indicated (for instance, John Merrick, of Malone, N.Y., might deed land in Derby, N.H., thus indicating a residence in Derby before he removed to Malone). Sometimes people went back to their original home to spend their old age, and you will find a deed indicating this— let us say that you find a deed in which Joseph Merrick, of Hannah, Mass., transfers his land in Derby. Sometimes, of course, a man was speculating in land and bought a lot of it in a town to which he never went— a link in my own ancestry is established by such a deed, for Samuel Hungerford, of New Fairfield, Conn., deeded land in Fairfield, Vt., to his daughter, Eunice Soule, and her husband, Joseph Soule, "for love."

To return to the case of the parentage of your great-grandfather, Jeremiah Merrick: suppose you find a deed in which Joseph Merrick, of Hannah, Mass., conveys his land in Derby to his son, Jeremiah, in 1830. Here you have pretty definite information that your Jeremiah was identical with the son of Joseph. You can picture the young man, married two years, making a go of it and receiving the farm on which he was living from his father who had removed to Hannah, Mass., by 1830. You still lack the birth record of Jeremiah, and perhaps his death record, but you are on the trail and no longer digging blindly. You still have probate records and cemetery records to help you establish your case.

About twenty-five years before Social Security made a central repository of vital records important to many people, most of the states had passed laws creating such an office and requiring that copies of all vital records be filed in a specified state office—sometimes the Health Department, sometimes the Department of Vital Records.

In many of the older states all vital records contained on the town books have been copied and sent to this central state office. These transcripts are made on cards, one for each individual record. The cards are generally filed in alphabetical order under the surname. In the *New England Historical and Genealogical Register,* Vol. 90 (January 1936), pp. 9–31, there is an article on the various state methods of keeping vital records, arranged by states. A digest of that article is to be found in Appendix B of this book.

In some states the law was made sufficiently inclusive to require that all cemetery records be included with the vital records from the town books (although in Vermont I find that this law has not been fully observed); and occasionally the law has directed that a transcript of church records as well be made.

By writing to the state office of vital records you can obtain all the information that is on file for, let us say, Jeremiah Merrick. For the official title and address of the appropriate office in each of the several states, get a copy of *Where to Write for Birth and Death Records* (Public Health Service Publication Number 630A) from the Superintendent of Documents, United States Government Printing Office, Washington, D.C. 20402. The price is 15 cents, but do not send stamps. This useful pamphlet will indicate how early the records in each state begin, give you the price for ordinary and certified copies, or, in certain instances, direct you to city or county offices for such records. No state office can be expected to supply an unlimited number of records—say you want all Merrick entries, births, marriages, and deaths—but will usually send you a list of local searchers. You select one and write for an estimate which is generally based on the time involved. Some searchers, from sad experiences, ask for payment in advance, others may rely on your honesty.

In a few states some of the vital records of the various towns have been printed. Massachusetts has taken the lead in this matter, thanks to the impetus given to the movement by individuals and privately endowed societies interested in genealogical and historical matters. The vital records down to 1850 of most of the towns in eastern Massachusetts, and many of those in the western part of the state, have been printed and are to be found in most genealogical libraries. The records of a few of the towns in Connecticut and Maine have been printed also. The vital records of scattered towns in other states have been printed in magazines, as appendixes to local histories, and occasionally at the personal expense of some interested individual or society.

The early land records of Suffolk County, Mass., have been printed and, in their black binding labeled "Suffolk Deeds," are familiar to many genealogists. Others have been abstracted and printed in whole or in part. The colonial documents of New York, Rhode Island, Plymouth Colony, and Massachusetts Bay Colony and the Providence, R.I., and Hartford, Conn., land records have been printed, to mention but a few. Most libraries having genealogical or historical collections own these volumes.

To return to the town offices, don't overlook the mortgage records, which, although they are not so frequently useful, do sometimes contain valuable clues.

Then there are tax lists, which provide a sort of census of the town, in that all taxpayers are listed. Since the federal census is taken every ten years only, these tax lists frequently serve as an intermediate census, and from them you can determine just when your people moved away from the town, or ceased to pay taxes, at least. You can figure out the size of their farms or how much land they owned and the value of it. Aside from definitely locating your people in that town, they help you to paint a picture of your family's standing and interests.

In some localities in the 1870's there were school censuses taken. In these were records of the heads of families and the names of children of school age in each family. If the vital records were poorly kept, these school censuses are valuable, because the age of each child was specified, and sometimes these records are more accessible to the searcher than the federal census records. They may or may not be valuable to you, but at least they are worth knowing about.

You may think that these various kinds of town records are as dry as the dust which so frequently covers them. But if you are on the watch for anything humorous, you will find many a funny thing in them. After all, these people were human, as even the dry old records show. There is one Connecticut marriage record, solemnly and seriously entered on the books and duly printed in a transcript, in which one John Boughton marries "I Dono Who"! Now it is quite obvious that the clerk did not know the name of the bride, perhaps forgot to ask it or had actually forgotten it when he came to make the entry on the books. Anyhow, I suspect that many a descendant of this couple has laughed off his irritation over this funny entry and searched elsewhere for the bride's name. Sometimes the clerk was not sufficiently interested to ask for such details. Sometimes he entered merely the sex of a child, as "a son" or "a daughter," whose birth he was recording, or the clergyman who performed the baptism forgot to write it down. Sometimes the spelling is quite phonetic, and you get curious names like "Febe" for Phoebe and "Kerrence" for Concurrence (I have once seen this spelled "Kurrants"). Alys and Ellis have been known for Alice. Joll has been used for Joel. Surnames are even worse when it comes to misspelling. Apostrophes were almost unknown, so sometimes an "s" was added to a name: for instance, Soule became Sowles, where the reference was to Soule's children or something of the sort. Sometimes the clerk didn't cross his "t" or dot his "i," and you get unintentional misspellings, such as Merrell for Merritt. The farther back you go, the more precarious the art of spelling becomes, so you must be always alert to catch it and never overlook a name because it isn't spelled exactly as you spell it today.

If it is not possible for you to go to the town clerk's office—if you live too far away and find it impossible to go halfway across a continent to consult the records—you have two means of getting at them. You may write to the clerk and ask him to find the record that you want and send you a copy of it; or you can employ a private searcher to go and examine the records in person—a relative, perhaps, or a professional genealogist.

Many town clerks are not especially interested in genealogy (all this fuss about ancestors seems trivial to them), so any search which they make is bound to be rather perfunctory and unsatisfactory. You must remember that your problem does not seem important to them and may even irritate them because it takes them from some more lucrative or pleasant occupation and makes it necessary to lift down those heavy volumes. Any such clerk is bound to be rather haphazard in his searching, and may easily 'overlook the record most important to you.

On the other hand, you may be fortunate in finding a clerk who is really interested in his records, has them completely and thoroughly indexed, and can give you accurate information. Such an official will frequently go out of his way to assist you and may refuse to accept any fee for his services. However, whichever type of clerk you find, my advice is that you should never accept a statement that such and such a record doesn't exist until you have had the opportunity to check it yourself or through another's service. Sometimes one eye will see what another had missed. But it doesn't pay to let the clerk know that you doubt his word, or to insist too much that he go over his records again. File his letter among your notes and make a mental memorandum, if not a written one, to go there sometime to take a look for yourself. But you might write to him again and ask him whether he searched the land records for any evidence bearing on your problem. Generally you can tell by the tone of his letter whether or not he has been very thorough. If the tone is brusque and abrupt or if he says that the records "seem" to contain no evidence, you may suspect that he merely "seemed" to search them. If he goes into details, you may have more confidence in his thoroughness.

In writing for records, you should always offer to pay any fee which the clerk may charge, and you will find it a good policy to enclose a self-addressed stamped envelope for reply. The fact that you are willing to pay for data will have a good effect upon him. Most people dislike those, particularly strangers, who are trying to get something for nothing, and many officials, particularly those living in small towns, object to being ordered about. Play up to them and make your need seem important to them, and impress them with the fact that you depend upon their good will and intelligence to help you solve your problem. It tickles their vanity, even though they may be shrewd enough to see through your ruse.

Moreover, in writing, always state your questions clearly and give all the information you can which will enable the clerk to make his search as easily as possible. Remember that he has many duties and may be a very busy man, without clerical help. He is more likely to serve you if your problem is clear and you ask for specific information. A demanding letter giving meager information, such as "I want the record of my great-grandfather, who lived in your town; please send it by return mail," will probably go into the wastebasket for it contains no names, no dates (even approximate), and no indication of what the ancestor's name may have been. Nobody unfamiliar with your problem can pull such information out of thin air. How is the clerk of whom you make this demand to know even the surname of the man whose birth record you require? He is far too busy to take the time to figure back four generations and decide that the man in question must have lived about a hundred years ago. Your chance of success would be much better if you wrote a letter like this:

> I am searching for the record of the parentage, birth, and marriage of my great-grandfather, Jeremiah Merrick, who is supposed to have married in your town sometime before 1835, and was probably born there between 1800 and 1810. I will gladly pay any fee which you may charge for a search of your records, and I enclose an envelope for your reply, which I hope to have at your convenience.

Don't be discouraged if the results of a search of the town records are very meager, for the sources of information are not exhausted, and you may yet solve your problem from other records.

For instance, there may be something in the county court records—I do not mean just the probate court, which will be discussed in Chapter Eight, but those mentioned on pages 93–95. Some lawsuits involve evidence of descent from the original grantee of the property in dispute, others may include testimony from relatives distant in ties of blood as well as in locality. By chance, in the papers accompanying such a case the very data you are looking for may be found, or a locality may be named with which you have never connected any of the family, and in the town clerk's office in that place you may find the records which you need to prove your descent. I know of one lawsuit which involved right of burial in a cemetery lot—a man sued his second cousin for burying the remains of an aged aunt in her grandfather's lot and tried to get a court order requiring that they be removed. He based his case on the fact that the deceased's mother had married and hence could no longer be considered a member of her father's family, but belonged in her husband's family; therefore her offspring was not entitled to space in her father's lot. In the evidence submitted there was quite of bit of genealogy of the family and a copy of the original owner's will, lost in the file of the probate court, was produced. It all made me think of J. P. Marquand's novel *The Late George Apley* and the amusing episode of the burial of Cousin Hannah's remains—if you enjoy a chuckle, look it up and read it.

CHAPTER SEVEN

Inscriptions in Cemeteries

PERHAPS NOWHERE is the transitory nature of the existence of human individuals brought home to us more vividly than in an old country graveyard which lies neglected and forgotten on a rural hillside. There are thousands of such burial grounds in the United States, each of them known only to comparatively few people, even among those living in the very town in which it is located. It frequently happens that no descendant of those whose remains are buried in such a cemetery is living near there today. In many other cases descendants living there do not care a tinker's damn about the condition of the almost forgotten family graves; or, to be more charitable, they are physically or financially unable to care for them. In some places the entire character of the population has changed and the old families have either died out entirely or moved away, to be replaced by recent immigrants who have no interest in the old burial places. Sometimes brush and brambles have grown so high that not a stone is visible when you first look at the thicket supposed to be the cemetery lot. Even a ten-foot obelisk may stand obscured from view by the dense young forest about it. Thus has the local fame of some proud old family been blotted out by nature's luxuriant growth.

Families once prominent in the community are now forgotten, even though their position and influence has been subtly indicated by the quality of the marble or granite marking their graves. In one town in northern Vermont I found the fine marble "table-slab" over the grave of the most prominent pioneer settler of the town

so weathered by the rains and snows of a hundred and
thirty-odd years that the long inscription, which presumably records his standing, has been obliterated beyond
recall. Yet the old volume recording the affairs of the
first quarter century of that town contains his name on
practically every page. Only an antiquarian, like myself,
and one or two others are aware that he played an important part in the establishment of the town, and I
doubt whether anyone besides myself knows where he
was buried. Not a person of his name lives in the town
today or has lived in it for a hundred years. Probably
95 percent of today's inhabitants of that town would not
recognize his name at all. *Sic transit gloria mundi!*

Such a circumstance is not peculiar to that particular
town but is duplicated in hundreds of others throughout
the country. We live in an age which has little respect
for the past and shows no inclination to profit by the
experience of those who have lived successfully and died
in peace.

Part of the explanation of this neglect of the old cemeteries is that the elements making up the population of
these old towns have changed radically during the last
century. Old stock and old families have died out, or
their descendants have moved away to the cities. "For-
eigners" have come in, bought up the old farms, gained
control of the town affairs, and, having no active, intimate interest in the past history of the town, have allowed the burial places of the town fathers to become
neglected. These, in the course of time, revert to natural
growth, for Nature, always fighting her children, has her
way unless there is a continual guard kept against her
ruthlessness.

Gravestones sink into the ground or fall down and get
broken by barbarians and vandals. The encroaching sod
soon covers them and they become buried beneath grass,
dead leaves, and broken twigs. Sometimes unfeeling human beings have picked up these old stones, carried
them away and used them as hearthstones, as doorsteps,
or as a part of the foundation of a new barn or out-
building, or for anything else for which a flat stone may
have been needed. Sometimes cows, breaking through an
old rail fence surrounding a cemetery or clambering over

a crumbling stone wall, have rubbed against the grave-stones and knocked them over, and then trampled them into the dirt.

Years later there comes along an ancestor hunter, look-ing for the records which those stones contain. On many occasions he must literally dig the records of his ances-tors out of the sod, and sometimes, if he has the means, he may restore the cemetery to some degree of order and have the stones reset. Or, when unable to bear the ex-pense of restoration, he carefully copies the inscriptions and preserves them in one way or another for the use of others searching for the data recorded on them.

In searching the cemeteries for the records of your forebears, the task is made easier if you can take an older relative with you, for frequently your grandfather, your great-uncle, or an old cousin can tell you about the relationships that existed between the individuals buried there. Sitting at home, they may not recall even the names of those who died so many years ago, but, when they are confronted with a memorial stone, the little bell rings in their minds and their memory is restored.

I recall trying, several years ago, to get a complete list of the children of my great-great-grandfather from my great-aunt. She knew that her father was one of twelve children, six boys and six girls. She could name eleven of them but could not recall the names of the sixth girl and her husband. We had the dates of birth from the eldest in 1791 to the youngest in 1817. As the six older children, whom she could remember, came along in 1791, 1795, 1797, 1799, 1801, and 1803, we felt confident that the missing girl was born in 1793, because, as my great-aunt remarked, "they had 'em every two years in those days." So, one fine afternoon, I helped Great-Aunt Elizabeth into the car and we drove to the cemetery where most of the family were buried. We began a systematic search of the yard, picking out the stones of all women whose births were indicated as occurring in 1793. We hadn't gone very far before I found a stone on which this in-scription stood: "Amanda, wife of Willis Northrop, died March 23rd, 1852, in her 59th yr." Sure enough, my great-aunt recalled her "Aunt Mandy" immediately, and we had the missing child!

But if you are not fortunate enough to be able to take your relatives to the cemetery and thus refresh their memory, you yourself can figure out (and later prove from other records) many of the relationships which you need for your record of the family. For instance, let us suppose that you are still trying to find the records of your great-grandfather, Jeremiah Merrick, and his wife, Hannah. You find in the cemetery their graves with stones reading like this:

Jeremiah Merrick   Hannah, Wife Of
1805–1851   Jeremiah Merrick
1808–1878

In your search of the town records you have already found that she was Hannah Lyon. Beside her here in the cemetery, you find a stone reading:

James Lyon
1770–1841

and on the other side of James, another:

Hannah
Consort Of
James Lyon
Died
May 3rd, 1838
In Her 66th Year

And perhaps beyond them, in the same lot, several children of James and Hannah Lyon, possibly two or three of them dying in maturity but apparently unmarried.

You would be justified in assuming that James and Hannah Lyon were the parents of Hannah, wife of Jeremiah Merrick. Your record of the marriage of Jeremiah Merrick to Hannah Lyon in 1828, and now the approximate date of her birth figured from her gravestone, together with the ages of James and Hannah Lyon at that time, indicate pretty clearly that they were her parents. This is further substantiated by the fact that your grandfather named a son James Lyon Merrick. Moreover, Hannah (Lyon) Merrick was obviously named for her mother, Hannah, "consort of James Lyon." James Lyon's will, or the administration of his estate, will probably prove your contention.

Perhaps in another lot, not far away or in an even older cemetery in the town, you find this inscription on an old slate stone:

Mary S., wife of
Joseph Merrick
Died
October 28th, 1805
In The 30th Year
Of Her Age

But you do not find beside her or in any other cemetery in the town the grave of her husband, Joseph Merrick (who, you may recall, was living in Hannah, Mass., in 1830, and may have been buried there). However, there are, in the lot with her, three small children, let us say:

Jeremiah
Infant Son Of
Joseph & Mary Merrick
Died
May 6th, 1801
Aged 6 w'ks

Mary
Daughter of
Joseph & Mary Merrick
Died
May 8th, 1801
Aged 2 y'rs

John
Son Of
Joseph & Mary Merrick
Died
May 1st, 1801
Aged 4 y'rs

Here you get a picture of what happened in that fateful May of 1801—an epidemic of smallpox, diphtheria, or scarlet fever sweeping through the town and hitting the Merrick family pretty hard, for they lost three small children, perhaps their entire family, within a week. Possibly the mother had it, too, and survived to die only four years later, probably soon after the birth of your Jeremiah, whom she named for the youngest boy that had died. Probably the John Merrick whose son Joseph was born in 1835 was another son, born in 1803 and named for the John who died in 1801; and perhaps the Henry you found was an elder son who survived the epidemic. Families in those days frequently repeated the names of deceased children, so anxious were they to have those names continued in the family. I know of four sons in one family who were given the same name, each after an older brother who died in infancy.

Sometimes it is well to examine the cemeteries in the towns which border on that in which your people lived. Boundary lines have changed, and land which was once in their town is now in another. Moreover, families marry back and forth, regardless of boundaries. Again, in northern Vermont, I know of four towns whose borders touch at one point. There is a graveyard in the point of one, within a stone's throw of the other three. In this cemetery are buried members of families who lived in three of those towns. There I found, after years of inter-mittent searching for his grave, the tombstone of the first husband of my great-great-grandmother. He died at the age of twenty-six—was killed in an accident which oc-curred in the sawmill in which he worked. Dying so young and within four years after his marriage, he was buried in his father's lot in that little cemetery. His widow married again, produced a large family for her second husband, and was buried beside that husband, nine miles away. You might assume from the inscription of the first husband's stone, and the absence of any wife beside him, that he died unmarried and was buried near his parents. Yet a large family developed through the only child of that early marriage. So it is not safe to assume too much from a single grave. Your genealogical intuition and your knowledge of conditions prevailing at the time in which these individuals lived must lead you to reasonable conclusions.

A century ago there were many more private ceme-teries than there are now. In frontier communities espe-cially, it was a frequent occurrence for people to be buried on their own land or at the edge of the clearings which they had made and were developing. Not many years ago I was prowling about on the back roads of my native town, searching for small cemeteries and isolated graves. I stopped to call on an old friend of my mother's and asked him if he knew about any graveyards or private burial grounds in that part of town. He told me that there was a gravestone in a small pasture near the house of his son-in-law, so we went over there and found it at the foot of a decayed apple tree which had long since passed its prime. The inscription read: "Bridget, wife of James H. Hawley, Esq., Died in August, 1791, aged 26 years & 3 months." That farm had been originally part of a large tract of land owned by Mr. Hawley, one of the pioneer settlers, who, together with another wife, was buried beneath an imposing monument in a cemetery in a neighboring town. Bridget, his first wife (she was born a Stanton), with whom he had shared the hardships of pioneering, lies forgotten beneath an old apple tree not far from the spot where they built their first cabin.

In working in old cemeteries you must really study the stones. Weathered inscriptions are difficult to read. Sometimes their legibility depends upon the light. If the sun is bright and the day is clear, the shadows may be sharp and easy to read. But if the sun's rays hit the stone at such an angle that no shadows are cast in the incisions on the stones, you must shade the stone, or the inscription, in such a way that you can read the letters. Sometimes, especially when you are attempting to photograph a stone, it is better to trace each letter of the inscription with common white chalk; in photographs the inscription always stands out much more clearly if this is done. Follow carefully the course of the engraving with your chalk in order that you may get all the lines, especially the fine lines. Sometimes it is easier to make a rubbing of the face of the stone. Take a large piece of wrapping paper, lay it flat against the stone, and rub over it with a soft lead or a piece of marking crayon, such as shippers use in marking packing cases—just as you, as a child, used to make rubbings of the front of your geography book when you were too bored in school to study.

Many different kinds of stones have been used for grave markers. These fall more or less into periods. Mrs. Harriette Merrifield Forbes's *Gravestones of Early New England and the Men Who Made Them, 1653–1800* (published in 1927) is an interesting study of the types of markers used before 1800. In the late eighteenth and early nineteenth centuries the stone commonly used was a soft, dark slate, which weathered easily and quickly and had a tendency to split off as the snow and ice worked on it in the wintertime or the rain soaked into its crevices in the summer. During this period the engravers used mainly a Roman letter, which is easily read if it has not weathered too much.

Between 1800 and 1850 a kind of grayish-blue slate was used. This is a harder stone than the dark slate and takes a better polish. But during this period the engravers used an Italic script for their lettering, which is sometimes very difficult to read. The heavy lines of the down strokes made by the engravers were cut deeply and have survived, but the hairlines of the cross strokes, such as most of the top of a figure 7 and the cross stroke of the elaborate 4, and sometimes the semihorizontal strokes of the 3's, 8's, and 9's, were lightly incised and on many stones these are almost or entirely weathered away. If the light isn't right, or your fingers aren't sensitive in tracing them, they are very difficult to see and read. Not infrequently a novice at reading gravestone inscriptions will misinterpret the figure 4 and read it as 11 or even 21 or 71, especially if the little horizontal stroke is obscured by a tiny bit of lichen or is not plain in the direct light of the sun, and the other figures of the date are illegible. Figures which are often confused are 8 and 3, while 9 in that script looks odd, and if the elongated tail has become obscured the figure may be mistaken for 0. The figure 1 was frequently made with an extended serif which can be read as a 7, thus throwing out calculations appreciably, and 2 is also confused with 7, especially if the lower tail is illegible. On a weathered stone 5 and 6, or 6 and 0 may be confused; and sometimes 3 and 5 are hardly distinguishable. A rubbing will sometimes solve the problem of reading.

So in reading the inscriptions on this type of stone and those of the period, 1800–50, you should be unusually careful to get an accurate transcription of the record. If you have any reason to question your interpretation of the figures, you should indicate that uncertainty with an interrogation mark and a note of what the alternative reading might be.

About 1840 or a little later a type of hard marble came into use and with it, perhaps because of its hardness, the use of Italic script began to wane and Roman lettering came back. Late in the nineteenth century granite came into popular use, and with it raised lettering, which unfortunately is sometimes as difficult to read as incised lettering, especially if the light isn't right or if lichen has grown over the stone. Within the last few years, the art of sandblasting an inscription into the stone has come into use. By this method the wording is cut in very deep, so it bids fair to stand a great deal of weathering and survive much longer than the old, hand-chiseled inscription.

Before 1850, gravestone inscriptions rarely contained inclusive dates, but generally the date of death followed by a statement of the age of the decedent. Sometimes this was given in years, months, and days: "Aged 87 yr's, 6 m's, & 3 d's." Given such an inscription, following the old rule which you learned in arithmetic, you can figure out the exact date of birth. But if you have an inscription such as "Aged 87 Years" your problem is not so simple. Only in extremely rare cases does a person die on the anniversary of his birth; consequently, whenever you find such an inscription, you may be reasonably sure that the odd months and days of the deceased's age were omitted from the inscription. Generally such an inscription implies that the decedent had passed his eighty-seventh birthday, but he may have been within a few weeks of it. You cannot tell from the inscription. If it reads: "Died April 25th, 1841, aged 87 years," he may have been born in 1753 or 1754, for his eighty-seventh birthday may have occurred some time after 25 April 1840 and before 1 January 1841, and hence he was born in 1753; or the birthday had occurred in 1841 before 25 April, or had been about to occur, and hence he was born in 1754. If you fail to find any evidence of the exact date of birth, you should always indicate the approximate date as, in this case, 1753–54.

It is equally difficult to figure birth dates from inscriptions which read like this: "Died May 1st, 1840, in the 26th year of his age." If a man was twenty-five in April 1840, he entered his twenty-sixth year at that time, and thus was born in 1815; on the other hand, if he had his twenty-fifth birthday after 1 May 1839, he was still in his twenty-sixth year when he died, but was born in 1814. So here again, failing other data, you must record the birth as 1814–15.

In copying inscriptions from gravestones it is always wise to copy *verbatim ac litteratim,* word for word and letter for letter, including all punctuation as it is given. This eliminates some of the chances for error. If a stone reads: "consort of," copy it that way, and do not substitute "wife" for "consort." "Consort" signifies that the husband (or, in rare cases, the wife) was living at the time, whereas "wife" does not necessarily have that meaning. "Relict" always means widow (although occasionally, widower); hence, in the absence of other evidence, you know that the wife survived her husband. It is a small point, but it sometimes has important significance. Of course, the introductory phrases, "In memory of" and "Sacred to the memory of," add nothing to one's knowledge, and they can be omitted without loss; but there is a difference between "in her 57th year" and "aged 57 years."

In the event of illegible inscriptions or portions of inscriptions, it is a good plan to enclose your interpretation of the illegible part in square brackets, thus [   ], when you make your transcription. This is a device used universally to indicate an editor's substitution for the original. Thus, any experienced person reading the following transcription:

[Sacre]d to the Memory of
[Jere]miah Merrick
[Wh]o Died
[Ja]nuary 24th 1841
[in] his 36th
[year]

would know that the inscription was partially illegible and that the copyist had supplied the portion enclosed

in the brackets, probably having made out enough of the
worn letters to be reasonably sure of what they were
originally.

This same device can be used to add a descriptive
phrase, thus:

> Hannah, Wife of
> Jeremiah Merrick,
> died
> August 1 [remainder of
> stone broken away]

While poking about in old cemeteries you come across
many sad things and many amusing things as well. There
are those, I know, who feel that it is very disrespectful
to the dead to find amusement in anything in a cemetery, but I hope that attitude is changing, for many of
the dead enjoyed gaiety in life and probably, if they
know anything about it, welcome a bit of it over their
resting places. Death can be beautiful or ludicrous, as
well as sad. The lugubriousness of the earlier attitude
toward it is amply expressed in the first line of the following epitaph from the gravestone of Eunice, wife of
Joseph Soule:

> Corruption, earth and worms
> Shall but refine this flesh
> Till my triumphant spirit comes
> To put it on afresh.

In the same cemetery, I found this epitaph on the
stone of Lewis Leach, who died in 1841:

> This modest stone, what few vain marbles can,
> May truly say, Here lies an honest man:
> Calmly he looked on either life and here
> Saw nothing to regret or there to fear.

There are nice implications in the following verses
from the marker of Clarissa Page (was she a sister of the
Cynthia Page, whose epitaph I quoted in Chapter One?
—they rest in different cemeteries in the same town):

> While sculptured marble speaks of fame
> And monuments o'er merit rise
> This stone shall to the world proclaim
> Tomb'd deep in earth here virtue lies.

And this in 1813, before the great Victoria was born!

Many people, some of whom are not even interested in digging for ancestors, collect epitaphs, make rubbings from seventeenth- and eighteenth-century gravestones, and plan their picnics and the spare moments of their vacations to include a cemetery, where they examine the old stones and copy what appeals to them.

In one cemetery I came across an orderly row of tombstones recording the existence of five of the wives of the patriarch who lay beyond them, with room left for the grave of the sixth, who survived him! In another I found, side by side, the graves of three sisters near those of their parents. These "Gilbert girls," as they were called, had a total age of more than 240 years and all died unmarried, carrying on their father's farm to the last. Near them were the "Olmstead girls," each of whom lived into her seventies. A telling indication of the New England tendency to spinsterhood!

Such inscriptions as these from a small remote village are not unusual. They can be duplicated in hundreds of others. Moreover, the discerning ancestor hunter can read the outline of the history of any town in its cemeteries. The changing types of names indicate the changes in the elements of the population. The rise and fall of families can be read in the simplicity and grandeur of the stones over their graves. Even the remnants of slavery can be noted, for I found in a small cemetery overlooking the Missouri River a simple marker of an old slave who was buried at the feet of a young woman whom she had nursed throughout a fatal illness.

Occasionally one finds a reminder of some very gruesome event. On a back road, in the town of Fairfield, Vt., there is a pasture in which, some hundred yards from the road, stands a small obelisk about three feet high. It is the memorial to Marrietta N. Ball, who was murdered near that spot in 1874. Sunken into it at one time was a daguerreotype portrait of Miss Ball, and below the identifying inscription was engraved a brief account of the manner in which she was killed: she was attacked while walking home from the school where she was teaching, her body was dismembered, and the torso was found on the spot where the monument stands. One other memorial stone of this kind is known to exist in the United States—somewhere in Rhode Island, I am told—but the type is more frequently found in England.

Although, as a general rule, a gravestone tells very little about the personal characteristics and history of the individual beyond the dates of the two major events in his life (birth and death), occasionally a stone gives a glimpse of the man he was. In a roadside cemetery within a mile of the eastern shore of Lake Champlain, I found the following inscription. It is not necessary to tell in more detail the story which it contains:

When true friends part
'Tis the survivor dies
. . . .
This Monument,
By a Beloved Friend Is
Erected to the Memory Of
JOSEPH R. FAY
Who Died On The 19th Of May
1803 in the 25th Year
Of His Age.
Thoughtful yet Smiling
. . . .
Farewell Bright Soul! A Short Farewell
Till we shall meet in realms above
In the sweet grove, where pleasures Dwell
And Trees of Life bear Fruits of Love.
. . . .
Could twin born Souls walk in hand!
Thro the dark shades of Death!
Vain Wish!

CHAPTER EIGHT

Where There's a Will There's a Way

THERE IS scarcely any legal record, containing names of individuals, which is not of use to a genealogist. The ancestor hunter who proposes to be thorough in his search and who wants as complete a picture of his ascendants as possible should by all means use all the records he can find. Some of them are of paramount importance in proving a descent; others are interesting only as they shed light upon the life and activities of the individual whom they concern.

Undoubtedly the most important evidence of the genealogy of a family is a collection of the probate court records which pertain to it. Wills are generally indisputable documents concerning the relationship of individuals, although occasionally they are exasperatingly meager in the information they give, and sometimes reveal more than the wording tells. Sometimes, on the other hand, they tell too much to suit the pride of the descendants. But the wise man knows that his ancestors were human beings with human attributes and shortcomings, and therefore he accepts them for what they were and tries to determine his heritage from them.

Each state has (and in colonial days each colony had) its own laws of probate. My knowledge and the space at my disposal are too limited to permit me to discuss here the differences in those laws, as they vary from state to state, or to consider the changes which have been made in them during the successive periods of American history. It is up to you, as an ancestor hunter keen on a find, to study the laws which affect the communities in which your ancestors lived, not only the probate laws, but the land laws and other laws governing the conduct of individuals. Although a great deal of digging can be accomplished without studying such laws, it is more fun and nets you a broader knowledge of the world if you have acquired some such knowledge.

There are two types of wills: the written will, signed and witnessed; and the spoken will, called the nuncupative will, generally given by the decedent on his deathbed in the presence of witnesses who are later called before the probate judge to swear to the testamentary intentions of the testator. The written will is by far the more common form today. In fact, nuncupative wills are rare in the twentieth century. But in the early colonial days, when writing material was not always at hand and a considerable proportion of the population could not write at all or wrote with difficulty even when in the best of health, nuncupative wills were much more common.

Wills have been known since pre-Christian times, and several truly ancient wills have survived, in tradition at least. The Bible (Genesis 48–49) mentions the will of Jacob, the Patriarch. Several wills are mentioned in the records of ancient Greece which have survived. But the oldest written will known to be in existence today in its original form is that of Sekhenren, an Egyptian. This will, dating from about 2550 B.C., was found by the late Sir William M. F. Petrie, the well-known Egyptologist, among some papyri which he excavated many years ago. It might easily have been drawn within the last century, so curiously modern is it in wording. The vocabulary of the law does not change so rapidly as language in everyday use. Sekhenren settled his property upon his wife, Teta, for life, and specified that his buildings should not be destroyed, although she was empowered to give them to any of her children. He even named a guardian for his infant children. This will was witnessed in the form of which our courts approve and contained an attestation clause very much like our modern clause of this sort.

English wills dating from the time of the Norman Conquest are common, and in the case of many the actual parchment on which they were written has survived. An interesting study of the wills of our English progenitors and those of our ascendants upon this side of the Atlantic

might be made, for they shed a great deal of light not
only upon the ownership and transfer of land but also
upon the kind of possessions which people have valued
from time to time and from period to period in history.
Old wills, English and American, frequently specified
what was to be done with such things as silver and
pewter, clothing, household utensils, books, and other
truly personal property. Today there is little respect for
personal property, but in colonial days, when "hard
money" was scarce, possessions were more important. A
piece of silver was greatly valued—it represented money;
a gun or a sword was precious and worthy of mention
in a will; a book was rare and truly treasured. Speaking
of books, the identity of the second wife of one of the
colonial ministers, the Reverend John Sherman, of Water-
town, Mass., is solved by a clause in the will of her
mother, Isabella (d'Arcy) (Launce) Simpson, who bequeathed her "great Bible" to her son-in-law in New
England.

In the seventeenth and eighteenth centuries, during
the period of the colonization of North America, many
wills contained bequests of rings or money for the purchase of a ring—"fifteen shillings for a ring," "ten shillings for a ring," were common phrases in the wills of the
well-to-do. This referred to what we call memorial rings.
They were finger rings, each to be worn in memory of a
deceased friend. Many of these memorial rings have survived. The late Sir Frederick Crispe made a large collection of them and published a descriptive catalogue of
them. Generally such rings were engraved with the name,
date of death, and age of the deceased. Sometimes they
were enameled, and coffins, death's-heads, spades, cross-
bones, and other symbols of death were worked into the
designs upon them. Generally such a ring was in the
form of a band, much like the old-fashioned yellow gold
wedding ring, but occasionally they were more elaborate.
I have seen one memorial ring, made late in the eighteenth century, in which a bit of the woven hair of the
deceased was set under glass, and held in place by pearls.
Izaak Walton, the famous fisherman, not only bequeathed
several such rings to his friends whom he wished to have
remember him, but indicated in his will the inscriptions

which were to be engraved upon them! Not long ago
there was found in Nebraska a memorial ring of Sir
Francis Nicholson, one of the colonial governors of Virginia, Maryland, and South Carolina.

This is but an indication of the byways into which you
may be led by the study of wills and testamentary bequests. William Hazlitt, the nineteenth-century English
essayist, has written a delightful essay, "On Will-Making,"
which is to be found in his volume *Table Talk, or Original Essays.* It will be well worth your time to read it,
for Hazlitt, a keen observer of human foibles, points out
some of the ridiculous aspects of wills and, incidentally,
comments in a pithy manner on human nature.

Seriously, however, the ancestor hunter must make an
extensive use of wills as he digs. The best plan is to visit
in person the probate office of the region in which your
people lived, and read thoroughly and with an alert mind
all wills which pertain to them although today photocopies made by Xerox or a similar machine save a lot of
trouble. A phrase, an apparently insignificant bequest, or
the mention of persons whose relationship to the legator
is not specified will frequently serve as the clue to further
digging. As a general rule the testator names his wife,
his sons in the order of their birth, and his daughters in
the order of age. This is especially true in wills made in
colonial times. The very wording of the will may indicate
clearly just how he felt toward each of them. "Cut off
with a shilling" is a popular saying, but it has more than
one implication in family history: possibly a previous
settlement upon that heir, or a retaliation for some offense
committed many years before, or a distrust of the lega-
tee's acumen or capacity to use property wisely. Today,
in America, the amount of such a bequest is generally a
dollar, or some sum which is ridiculously small in com-
parison with the size of the estate or the shares of the
other heirs.

Not long ago I read the will of a woman who survived
her husband a great many years and managed the property which he left her with acumen and sagacity. Her
estate was of considerable size, and in her original will
she mentioned by name all of her surviving children and
grandchildren, bequeathing to each of them a just share

of her property. A few years after the will was written, signed, and witnessed, she added a codicil in which she revoked her bequest to the widow of one of her sons and gave explicit reasons for her action. Knowing that any money left to the children of that son (they were all minors) would, by hook or crook, soon be squandered by their mother, she cut off those children, as well, and stated that the reason for such unnatural action was the "vile" character of their mother. Such a will arouses wonder, especially when it is known that the testator's reputation for a kindly disposition and a lovable character, albeit companioned by a strong, shrewd mind, has survived her these many years.

Wills are generally considered to be a source of proof of descent rather than of ascent, but occasionally the parentage of the testator, even though he was an old man, is given in the will. Several years ago I was tracing a Randall line back to the immigrant. I was "stuck" with a Joseph Randall, whose gravestone I had found bearing the information that he "died February 22nd, 1822, aged 67 years." I had found out that he was a Revolutionary soldier, and that he had a pension for his service as such. The pension records in Washington stated that he was born in Canada and enlisted first in 1775 from "Saint Tour" (which is Saint Ours, near Richelieu, Quebec). They also gave the date of his marriage to Judith Bowen in Lebanon, N.H. Finally I did what I should have done earlier—went to the probate office to search for his will. To my great pleasure and astonishment, he had disposed of any property which might be due him from the estate of *his father*, Michael Randall, and implied that that estate was in "Lower Canada," as Quebec used to be called. The will was exasperating in another aspect, however, because he mentioned none of his children by name and left all his property to his widow with the request that she divide "equally among our youngest children" anything that should remain at the time of her death.

Wills are not the only records or documents to be found in a probate office which are of use to a genealogist. Next in importance to a will is the distribution of an estate. Such a document shows just what proportion of the estate went to each heir, and each heir is generally named. Frequently the relationship of the heirs to the decedent is shown as "son John" and "daughter Jane" are assigned their respective shares. When a person has died intestate, that is, without leaving a will, the distribution is made in accordance with the law governing cases of the sort. In such an event, owing to the absence of a will, the record of distribution becomes a very important document to the ancestor hunter. I know of one distribution in which over twenty heirs are named and the amount given to each is specified, although the relationship is not specifically stated. The deceased died intestate without children, so his widow received one-third, and the remaining two-thirds of his estate was divided among the surviving brothers and sisters and the heirs of those who had predeceased him. By carefully adding the amounts received by the several groups of heirs it is possible, with a little trouble, to figure out which were which in relationship to the deceased and to the surviving brothers and sisters. This distribution proved to be of great value in determining the number of children of the deceased's father who grew to maturity, married, and produced offspring, and it helped me considerably in tracing the descendants of one branch of a family the genealogy of which I was compiling. A little common sense and a little experience in using such a record will enable you to get a great many clues from a document of this sort.

In the old days, a guardian for minor children—even though one parent survived—had to be selected and appointed by the judge of probate; in some states this is still true. The records of such appointments not only indicate relationships but sometimes contain a commentary indicative of the conditions existing within the family. In colonial days, and even later, children of fourteen were allowed to signify their acceptance of the guardian chosen by the judge, or, when they reached that age, were permitted, with the consent of the court, to choose a new guardian. Hence, a widow might be appointed guardian of her young children, and one of them, say a son, upon reaching the age of fourteen might choose his uncle or even a friend as his guardian, in lieu of his mother. This frequently happened when the mother had married again.

Guardianship papers are also filed for defectives and for old people who have passed into senility and are no longer capable of managing their own property. Not a few scandals have arisen over such cases and sometimes it is necessary to refer to the records of courts other than probate courts (orphans' courts, for instance) for more complete data in connection with them. Jurisdiction over such cases varies in the several states, so you should talk with some lawyer concerning their legal aspects, or yourself, in your search for further information, make a study of the law.

Most amateurs, and many professional genealogists, completely overlook other types of legal court records in their search for ancestors. However, buried in the files of innumerable courts throughout the country are depositions, records of lawsuits, and other court actions which teem with clues to the identity of those who have lived in the past—your ancestors and mine. There are printed indexes to the "reports" of the several states—the long series of printed volumes of cases which have been tried in the courts and "reported" for the use of other lawyers seeking precedents for their arguments and briefs. As a general rule, the documents cited are not printed in full but merely abstracted or summed up, so from the printed reports you get just the pith of what they contain. An examination of the actual documents in the files of the court in which the case was tried will frequently give you much more information and you may even obtain certified copies of the original records which were filed with those documents at the time the case was tried. Quite naturally and as you would expect, lawsuits over the distribution of estates, and contests of wills, are of the most value to the ancestor hunter. But I found valuable data in a suit against an insurance company in Wisconsin and still more in a contest over the ownership of some land in central New York. The records of criminal trials, especially murder cases, frequently produce evidence of a relationship for which other records cannot be found.

These more miscellaneous types of court records which

are mentioned here should be searched in person, either by yourself or by a competent genealogist whom you have hired to do the searching for you. The clerk of such a court, unaccustomed to this use of the records in his custody, will hardly know how to get from them the details which you wish, for, as a general rule, he has no knowledge of the data which a genealogist requires.

But probate records and transcripts or abstracts of other documents connected with the settlement of an estate can be secured by correspondence. The clerks of probate courts are all accustomed to receiving letters from all parts of the country asking for information contained in wills, inventories, and distributions. When a fee established by law is paid, it is, in many states, the duty of the probate clerk to furnish certified copies of wills or other papers pertaining to the settlement of an estate. Many probate clerks will undertake to make abstracts, especially if paid for it, but this is generally a private arrangement between you and the clerk. Usually there is someone in the probate office who is willing to augment a slender salary in this way. If you order a certified copy, it is always wise to find out in advance how much it is going to cost you—some wills are lengthy documents! Also, you should be sure that it will contain what you are looking for, since many testators have been exasperatingly reticent about their children's names. I have found that it is generally wise to word your initial query something like this: "Is there on file in your office the will of John Doe, who died about 1821? Or an agreement of his heirs? Or any other paper which makes mention of his daughter, Mary Jones? If so, can you supply an abstract, and how much would that cost?" Be sure to give the probate office some idea of the date of the instrument for which you are searching, for there may be two or three or more John Does, all of whom left wills. If you are not at all certain of the date of death, ask him to give you the dates of the wills which are on file in his office—in the light of your other clues they may mean something to you.

Sometimes, when you are trying to determine the parentage of some ancestor, it is feasible to have the clerk examine all the wills made by persons of that surname

which are on file in his office. Possibly he can do this at
his leisure and tell you whether your ancestor, or anyone
of his name, is mentioned in any of these wills. Suppose,
for instance, that you know that your great-grandfather
was born in Cabell County, W. Va., and have come upon
a tradition that was ten years old when his father died.
You could write to the probate clerk of that county, give
him such clues as you have, and ask if a child of his
name was mentioned in the will of any of the same surname who died about 1808–10, let us say, and offer, of
course, to pay for a copy or an abstract of the will in
which he was mentioned. Frequently a clerk will go out
of his way to obtain the data that you want. Once, while
examining in person the records of a probate court, I
found that the clerk was descended from the individual
whose will I was seeking. On the slender claim of cousinship, he practically turned the place upside down in
helping me and used his intimate knowledge of the records under his jurisdiction greatly to my advantage.
(And, of course, to his own, for whatever he found to
aid me gave him so many more data for himself. I have
often wondered whether he became thoroughly inoculated with the genealogical virus and went on with his
digging.)

Although the names of testators are indexed in the
probate court files, the names of persons mentioned in
wills are not indexed. Would that every probate court
ordered such an index made! It would be of great assistance to us genealogists. Frequently we are searching
for the identity of some ancestor's wife whom we know
only by her given name. In innumerable cases the will of
her father, could we but find it, would prove her identity.
But it takes a great deal of time and patience to read
through volume after volume of crabbed old handwriting
in the hope of finding her mentioned in some will. If we
had an index to the legatees, witnesses, and other individuals mentioned in testaments and distributions, our
work would be much simpler, although perhaps not quite
so thrilling.

It is a good plan to find out just what the probate
court is called in the state in which you are searching,
particularly if you are working by correspondence, for

the names differ in some states. Most states call the repository for wills and other probate records the probate office, or probate court. But in New York, for instance, it is called the surrogate's court, because it is in the charge of a surrogate. Moreover, in some states the limits of the probate district do not correspond with the county limits, although generally they do and you will find the probate records kept in the county court house. There are sometimes exceptions even within states. For example, in Vermont, although many of the probate districts correspond with the counties, there are twenty probate offices and only fourteen counties. Occasionally the limits of a probate district have been changed in the course of time, so it becomes necessary to learn something about the history of the district.

Incidentally, many states issue, generally through the office of the secretary of state, a manual in which are listed all state and county officials. In many states this manual can be obtained for the asking. There certainly is no harm done in applying for it. If you do get it you will have definite information about where and to whom to write for your data.

For instance, there is an unofficial annual publication for Vermont, first issued in 1818 as *Walton's Vermont Register,* now called *The Vermont Year Book* (published by the National Survey, Chester, Vt.). It contains, in alphabetical order, a list of all the towns, cities, and villages in the state. Under each town it gives its location, area, elevation, population, officers, manufacturers, merchants, churches, pastors, lawyers, postmaster, etc. In the introductory section the state and county officers are listed, as well as schools, colleges, and other institutions and organizations. There is usually a folded map of the state included. Such a handbook is useful to the ancestor hunter and should be consulted in your search.

Incidentally, a useful book, compiled with painstaking care by Noel C. Stevenson, of Waso, Calif., a Fellow of the American Society of Genealogists, is *Search and Research* (1959) which tells you under the heading "Official Records" where the probate offices are located and gives you many other valuable addresses. It is arranged by states and is easy to use.

CHAPTER NINE

What You Can Find in the Church Records

LONG BEFORE the earliest colonists came to America, it
had become the custom in most European countries to
keep records of the members of the ecclesiastical parishes. In fact, in England there was an Act of Parliament
passed in 1538, requiring the clerk of each parish to keep
a register of all marriages, christenings, and burials which
occurred within his jurisdiction. In many of the English
parishes these records have survived from the sixteenth
century to the present day, although innumerable volumes have been destroyed by fire or lost by careless
custodians. While in England in 1932, I personally examined the register of St. Helena's parish in the little
village of Tarporley, Cheshire, and found that it was
practically complete from 1548 to the present. Nearly
four hundred years of marriages, christenings, and burials in that old Cheshire parish—what a wealth of genealogical material! Incidentally, many of these old English
parish registers have been published, either by private
individuals interested in preserving such records or by
societies organized for that purpose, so it is possible for
us to use them in some of the larger libraries here in
America.

Although for a while our forebears in this country,
particularly in New England, did not recognize as legal
the ecclesiastical ceremony of marriage—the colonies of
Plymouth and Massachusetts Bay were especially anxious
to get away from the authority of the official church, to
separate church and state, as it were—nevertheless, the
hundreds of volumes of church records extant, dating

98

from the earliest colonial days, are of inestimable value to the ancestor hunter. Buried in them are many records without which his problems would be even more serious than they actually are.

It is interesting to note that, religious as the Puritans are reputed to have been and were, they considered marriage not as a religious sacrament, but as a civil contract. A marriage ceremony was performed before a magistrate. In fact, at one time ministers of the church were *forbidden* to perform a marriage. Hence, although you will find baptisms and burials recorded in the record books of the old churches, you will not find the early marriages entered there. But "intentions" of marriage may be found in church records since "publication of banns" in the church preceded the civil ceremony. Sometimes, however, there was a slip; the "intention" was not fulfilled and each of the parties married someone else! Study the baptismal records of the children and note the mother's name (if both parties are mentioned, as they generally were if both were members of the church). If there is a change in the mother's name between, say the fourth and fifth children, it is an indication of the death of the first wife and the remarriage of the father, even though the spacing between the children may not be more than the usual two years—in those days, when a wife was an economic necessity, they didn't always wait a "respectable" period! Young children had to be cared for, fields had to be tilled, meals had to be cooked, wool had to be carded, spun, and woven: a man could not do everything! So, be alert for any change in marriage partners.

Sometimes a man and his wife were not admitted to the church until after several children had been born— perhaps they did not settle in that town until some time after their marriage, or perhaps they did not realize what it meant to them spiritually or socially to be members of a church. Respectability in those days was closely allied to church membership and religious belief. Frequently you will find the baptismal record of a family of two adults and four or five children on a single page of the church records, perhaps following the record of the admittance of the parents to membership.

Sometimes, especially in pre-Revolutionary records, you will find children baptized "in the name of" one parent or the other. This generally means that that parent was a member of the church while the other was not, although, if the record of the admittance of both parents to membership has been found, it may mean simply that one parent was absent from church the day on which the child was presented for baptism. If, however, the record reads:

> Admitted to the Ch. Clarissa Smith and baptized for her four children, John, Seth, Sarah and Clarissa.

you may be sure that Clarissa's husband did not become a member at that time, and perhaps never did. In rare instances, when the record of the admittance of both husband and wife to the church is given and then the baptism of a child is recorded in the name of the wife only, it may be an indication that the paternity of the child was in question.

Church records, unlike town records, are not always easy to locate. They were generally kept by the minister himself, or, more recently, by a clerk. As few churches had offices for the minister in the church building, the record books were kept at the home of the minister (or some other individual) who had charge of them. Sometimes the pastor moved on to another charge and took the records with him, perhaps through oversight. Sometimes they got back to his successor, sometimes they did not. Many of them have been destroyed by fire or flood, many of them have been mislaid or lost, and occasionally some of them have been inadvertently destroyed in other ways. Occasionally they have been deposited for safekeeping in some secure place and forgotten. This is especially true in the case of churches which have gone out of existence in older communities. I have been looking for years for the records of a church in my native town, which was once Methodist and then Baptist and then a "union" church. Each person to whom I talk knows that there are records, but no one can say just where they are.

Sometimes the state organization of the church or religious society has gathered into its keeping the older records and those of the abandoned churches. In many cases, in the older states, state historical societies have become the custodians of the records of many of the churches, particularly those no longer active, which exist or have existed within their borders. In Connecticut, and undoubtedly in many other states, the State Library has gathered into its fireproof vaults many of the ancient church records of the state and stands ready always to accept the custody of more. In Vermont the Vermont State Historical Society has obtained possession of many such records.

Some of the church historical societies have actively collected the records of their denominations. For example, at the Colgate-Rochester Divinity School, Rochester, N.Y., the American Baptist Historical Library contains many invaluable records pertaining to the activities of the Baptist Church in North America—both manuscript and printed. Incidentally, in this connection it is valuable to know that the Baptists were organized into associations, covering several towns. These associations held annual or biennial meetings, and frequently the proceedings were published and a list of the official delegates was printed with the proceedings. These printed proceedings, collected at Rochester, are truly a source of data for the ancestor hunter—especially the list of delegates contained in them.

The Drew Theological Seminary in Madison, N.J., has a collection of historical material pertaining to the Methodist Church.

Those interested in the records of the Roman Catholic Church should consult Cora C. Curry's *Records of the Roman Catholic Church in the United States as a Source of Authentic Genealogical and Historical Material* (Washington, 1935; National Genealogical Society Publication No. 5). The records of the Episcopal Church are retained in the parishes, but the records of abandoned missions and parishes will be found in the diocesan offices. The American Jewish Archives, Cincinnati, Ohio, and the American Jewish Historical Society, New York, have large collections of historical material.

One great difficulty in locating church records arises

when the church is of the "mission" type, that is, the pastorate is supplied from a neighboring church or congregation. Sometimes there is a clerk who has charge of the records, but quite as often the records are kept by the clergyman who supplies the pulpit, and hence he carries them with him or, worse yet, makes the record of a baptism or marriage when he gets home from the service, if he happens to remember to do it.

Some ministers kept private record books and carried them about with them as they served one charge after another. This was especially true of Methodist circuit riders, who traveled constantly from one group of communicants to another. The heirs of these ministers have sometimes preserved such record books; but more frequently, I fear, the records have been destroyed as worthless or lost during the migrations of the family. These are generally nineteenth-century records, but they cover a period which the genealogist experiences difficulty in bridging. It is sometimes much harder to find the records of the generations between 1775 and 1850 than it is to find those covering 1620 to 1775. Moreover, the period between 1800 and 1870 was one of great migration—the West was being opened up for settlement. Pioneer settlements were not organized to keep vital records. Marriage licenses were scarcely known. The itinerant minister sometimes had several ceremonies to perform on one of his rare visits to the community. Hence, his record, if he kept one, is sometimes the only source of data—and it is very difficult to find that marriage book. Whenever you do find such a volume in private hands, you should make every effort possible to secure it for deposit in a historical or genealogical library, or should urge its owner so to deposit it. Failing in this, you should attempt to secure a careful and accurate transcript or microfilm of it and publish or deposit that transcript. By so doing you can greatly help other ancestor hunters, and save someone else the time which you have spent in your search for the records.

One collection of genealogical records kept by a religious organization, which is of great importance (undoubtedly the largest in the world), is that at Salt Lake City, in the offices of the Church of Jesus Christ of

Latter-day Saints, popularly known as the Mormon Church. In 1930 when I stopped in Salt Lake City to consult the genealogist of the Sherwood family about a problem in my ancestry, she suggested that I visit the church offices and obtain permission to consult these records. I was amazed at what I found there—over five million names in a huge card file, which serves as an index to thousands of sheets of family records. It is a part of the belief of the members of this church that the family is a unit in the future paradise, and "living children have a distinct obligation, therefore, to seek out the records of their progenitors, proving carefully the connections between one generation and the one beyond it, and to trace these genealogical lines as far back into the past as they can be authentically proved." Hence the members of that church are "extremely solicitous to obtain the names and full identification of the husband, wife, and of all the children, even those who died in infancy." (I quote from a letter of the late Archibald F. Bennett, the secretary of the Genealogical Society of Utah.)

This accounts for the presence of these records in Salt Lake City. Innumerable Bible records, records from old family hymnals, account books, and diaries, records from the memories of members of that church who died fifty, seventy, eighty years ago—perhaps extending back a century or more—and records from many other sources have been preserved in clear and concise form in this great repository. Some of them have been copied from printed sources, but by far the greater number of them are copies of unprinted records. In fact the Church has a tremendous project underway whereby the records of towns, cities, counties, parishes, churches, and private organizations in the United States and Europe are being copied on microfilm and filed in Salt Lake City. In 1972 the collection consisted of nearly a million reels, kept in huge vaults tunneled into a mountain of solid granite high in a canyon outside Salt Lake City; it is growing by about 50,000 reels a year as more records are filmed. In it are films of hundreds of English parish registers from which the Genealogical Society is making typewritten copies, arranged in alphabetical order, very carefully

read and checked for errors, and then bound in folio
volumes. The Society cannot consult these for you, but
the director of research will supply a list of accredited
genealogists who are competent to search a given parish
register for you.

The records of the Quaker meetings are being published as the *Encyclopedia of American Quaker Genealogy,* which has already been mentioned (see page 58).
The Friends keep very careful records of all their members, their births, marriages, and deaths, as well as transfers from one meeting to another. In using Quaker records you should remember that they use numbers to
refer to months and days of the week. Generally the
number representing the month is given first, the day
second, and then the year of our era, thus: 1–9–1777,
meaning January 9, 1777. A Friends marriage record, or
certificate, will be signed by all those present; hence it
has unusual value to the genealogist.

Church records contain more of interest to the ancestor hunter besides marriages, baptisms, and burials. Frequently the records of the transference of members,
generally by "letter," to another congregation serve as
valuable clues to migration; and, vice versa, the admittance of new members by "letter" from another church
will enable you to trace a migrating ancestor back to his
former residence. As an example, one church record book
contains these data: "Admitted to this Ch. Lewis Gilbert,
by letter from the Ch. in Cornish." This leads the digger
to another state and another source of information—the
town records and the church records of Cornish. Membership lists are sometimes annotated with data added
in a later handwriting. Words, such as "dec'd" (for deceased) or "removed," have been written into the mar-
gins, generally by a later clerk who was revising the
membership list. Dates are sometimes added to these
notes, thus, possibly, giving you the date of an individual's death, for which you have found no other proof.

Once in a while you will find "excom," or some similar
abbreviation, written in. To my astonishment, I found
several such notes on the membership list of a certain
Congregational church. I had never before known or
heard that the Congregational Church sometimes excom-

municated members, but as I leafed through the records of that church I found several lengthy accounts of excommunication trials. One man and his wife were tried on several counts, back about 1819, and were finally declared excommunicated from the church for blasphemous language, failing to attend church on Sunday, and nonsupport of the church. Verbatim reports of some of the evidence made very interesting reading, and from these reports I gained a very vivid picture of the family life of this couple. The dignified and righteous old deacons reported the names which they had heard each call the other, and also the opinion which each had expressed of the other. Moreover, the record of this same trial gave me considerable insight into the rivalry existing at that time between the two Protestant churches in the town, for it seems that there had been some proselytizing by the other church and its members had told these backsliders what they thought of the tenets of the "Society" (Congregational) to which the defendants belonged. One can imagine the gossip at afternoon tea parties on the front porches, that summer of 1819, and the sanctimonious awe with which some of the words and phrases were repeated—in quotation, of course!

Amusement aside, however, church records are far too valuable to be overlooked when you go digging for ancestors. You should make every effort to find them and use them, even if you have to go through them page by page in search of the records of your ancestors.

CHAPTER TEN

Government Aid in the Search

MANY RECORDS to be found in the archives of the government of the United States are of great value to those who dig for ancestors. From the earliest days of its existence, even during its provisional period, the federal government has been accumulating records which quite naturally pertain to individuals. Among the earliest of this kind are the payrolls of the troops serving in the Continental Army during the Revolutionary War. These are of value to persons who wish to establish membership in the Daughters of the American Revolution, the Sons of the American Revolution, and the other organizations, called "patriotic societies," in which membership is based on a descent from a patriot of that period. Some of the later records are, however, of more general interest.

Probably the most important of the records in the National Archives in Washington are those gathered by the census takers every ten years. The first federal census was taken in 1790 and was probably ordered by Congress for the purpose of determining the possible military strength of the nation. The returns of this census were published by the Bureau of the Census in 1909 in twelve volumes known to genealogists as the 1790 census. I quote from the introduction to one of those volumes:

> The First Census of the United States (1790) comprised an enumeration of the inhabitants of the present states of Connecticut, Delaware, Georgia, Kentucky, Maine, Maryland, Massachusetts, New Hampshire, New Jersey, New York, North Carolina, Pennsylvania, Rhode Island, South Carolina, Tennessee, Vermont, and Virginia. . . . A complete

set of the schedules for each state, with a summary for the counties, and in many cases for towns, was filed in the State Department, but unfortunately they are not now complete, the returns for the states of Delaware, Georgia, Kentucky, New Jersey, Tennessee, and Virginia having been destroyed when the British burned the Capitol at Washington during the War of 1812.

It was found, however, that partial returns for Virginia were available in the state's own enumerations (called "tax lists") of 1782, 1783, 1784, and 1785; so it was possible to reconstruct for Virginia a list comprising "most of the names of heads of families for nearly half of the state." These lists were printed in 1909 to form the Virginia volume of the set.

Thus we have printed schedules for Connecticut, Maine (originally taken as part of Massachusetts), Massachusetts, Maryland, New York, North Carolina, Pennsylvania, Rhode Island, South Carolina, Vermont, and Virginia, in which are listed the heads of families living in those states in 1790. The returns for South Carolina were not all in until March 1792, because the marshal for that state had difficulty in finding enumerators who would work for the salary which the government was authorized by Congress to pay. Since Vermont was not admitted until 1791, the actual census in that state was not taken until April–September 1791. For a list of schedules on file, and those missing, see Appendix C.

In addition to those volumes, the Bureau of the Census published, also in 1909, an analysis of this census, called *A Century of Population Growth from the First Census of the United States to the Twelfth, 1790–1900,* which forms a useful supplement frequently overlooked by genealogists and ancestor hunters. There are two particularly valuable features of this supplement. The first is the series of maps showing the development of the country from 1790 to 1900, especially useful because of the indication of the boundary lines of the various counties of the several states and the changes which have been made in them from time to time. The second useful feature is the lengthy table of names found in the census schedules in 1790, showing just what spellings were used for each name in the different schedules. This list, called "Table 111," is found on pages 227–70 of this volume, and is worthy of careful study, for only a few names achieved the distinction of uniform spelling in this census. Those are generally monosyllabics like Fox, Gage, etc., which even a census taker could not help spelling correctly. A complex name like Fitzgerald appears in twenty-four different spellings, including one so strange looking as Fitsjerald. Even so simple a name as Smith is found in nine different spellings.

The instructions issued to the 650 "marshals" who took this census directed them to list the heads of families by name and note the number of individuals living in each of the families in the following five classifications: (1) free white males, sixteen years and upwards, including heads of families; (2) free white males under sixteen years; (3) free white females, including heads of families; (4) all other free persons; and (5) slaves. The "all other free persons" comprised white people who were not considered heads of families (for instance, in Exeter, N.H., Joel Gill is so listed, but was not considered a "head of a family," although the census, following his name, noted three "free persons"—apparently himself and two others); free colored persons; and possibly a few Indians.

The amateur ancestor hunter who has traced his lineage back to 1800 or a little before will find these printed volumes of the 1790 census a mine of information and a source of clues which can be followed up in further searching. Let us suppose that you are tracing a Pangbourne line, and that Grandfather Pangbourne has told you that his people came from Vermont. You know from the records he has given you that his father, whom we will call John Pangbourne, was born about 1788–89, presumably in Vermont. You are searching for a clue to his parentage, so you consult the 1790 census for Vermont. Here you find that Stephen and Samuel Pangbourn and Timothy Pangborn were heads of families in the town of Addison, Addison County, Vt., in 1790 (1790 census, Vermont, p. 11); that Samuel and Joseph Pangbone were heads of families in Ferrisburg, Addison County, Vt. (1790 census, p. 12); and that Jesse Pangbowen was the head of a family in Fairfield, Chittenden County, Vt. (1790 census, p. 24).

The differences in the spelling of the surname should be ignored, for two reasons. In the first place, spelling was precarious at that time: men even signed their own names with different spellings on different occasions; or a clerk frequently spelled the name as he heard it pronounced rather than be bothered with asking how to spell it. The other reason is that these census records were printed more than 125 years after they were written, so the paper and ink have faded, fine strokes of the pen have worn away as the pages have rubbed against each other in use, and the clerks, expert as they were in reading old documents, have occasionally erred in interpreting the several handwritings in which these records were written. Hence, although the name was printed "Pangbowen" or "Pangbone," an examination of the original record in Washington might show that the name was actually written "Pangbourn" and was misinterpreted by the clerk who prepared the copy for the printer. Or, the marshal who made the enumeration in Ferrisburg or the one who made it in Fairfield did not catch the soft Vermont slur of the "r" and understood the name as "Pangbone" or "Pangbowen."

Of these heads of families named Pangbourne (in its several spellings) one, Jesse, can be eliminated immediately, for the time being at least, for his family consisted of but two males over sixteen, no boys and no females. It is possible that he had left his family somewhere else and, with a man to help him, was preparing a home in Fairfield at that time. But we will not consider that possibility in this instance. Thus your search is narrowed down to Stephen, Timothy, and Samuel in Addison, and Joseph and Samuel in Ferrisburg, each of whom had in his family a male or males under sixteen—your hypothetical John Pangbourne would have come in this classification if he had been born in 1788–89.

You will note that, through the use of this census, you have been able to narrow the field of your search down to two towns in Addison County, Vt. So you are in a position to go ahead, searching the vital records in those towns, the wills and other probate records in that probate district, etc., for evidence that one of these five men was the father of your great-grandfather. In writing to the town and probate clerks you ought to leave nothing to chance, and therefore should mention the various spellings of the name that you have found in the census records.

Possibly the 1800 census might be of further assistance to you. The Vermont Historical Society has published that Vermont census from a photostat copy which has been in its possession some time. From this we learn that there were only two Pangborn families then residing in the state: Reuben Pangborn at Panton, Addison County, with two males under ten, one male between ten and sixteen, one male between twenty-six and forty-five (without question Reuben himself), one female under ten years, one between ten and sixteen, and one between twenty-six and forty-five; and Stephen Pangborn, still in the town of Addison, with one male between sixteen and twenty-six, and one over forty-five (undoubtedly Stephen himself), two females between sixteen and twenty-six, and one female over forty-five (probably Mrs. Stephen). Either your hypothetical John had migrated elsewhere with his father's family or he was the son of Reuben Pangborn.

None of the schedules for the censuses after 1790 have been printed by the government, although they are all on file in Washington (a few schedules, such as the Alabama schedule for 1800, have been lost or destroyed). In order to use them one has to have them searched in Washington. Such a search is not so very expensive, and it may produce results very useful to you. Frequently, by searching these later census records you can trace the progress of a family, either as the children mature, marry, establish families of their own, and come to be listed as heads of families, or as they disappear from the records of one town and appear in those of another. You can determine the approximate date of the death of a man as his name disappears from the census records. If he died young, frequently his widow is listed as the head of the family in the next census—not a few women appear, even in 1790, as heads of families consisting, generally, of minor children.

As an example of the use of successive censuses, let us take a bona fide case this time, in which the only records used are those obtained from the censuses themselves. John Castle (or Castel, as his name was spelled in some of the census records) was a resident of Fairfield, Vt., and first appears there as head of a family in the 1810 census, when his family consisted of one male aged between twenty-six and forty-five, two males under ten, one female between twenty-six and forty-five, and two females under ten. By using our heads and a little arithmetic we can figure out that he was born between 1765 and 1784 (if he was aged between twenty-six and forty-five in 1810); since all the children were under ten, he was probably married about 1799 or 1800, or perhaps a year later than that (allowing a year after marriage before the birth of the first child, and two years between the births of the other three). As neither he nor any other man of the name of Castle was listed in the 1800 census of Fairfield, we know that he must have settled there some time after 1800 and probably was not married there. So we begin to get a picture of his family.

In 1820 his family, as enumerated in the census of that year, consisted of one male between twenty-six and forty-five, two males between ten and sixteen, three males under ten, one female between twenty-six and forty-five, one female between sixteen and twenty-six, one female between ten and sixteen, and two females under ten. Now we can narrow his birth date down to some time between 1775 and 1784 (he was still under forty-five in 1820); moreover, he now has nine children (unless the female between sixteen and twenty-six was a hired girl helping his wife, or some other dependent, which is unlikely in so clear-cut a case as this).

In 1830, as the census of Fairfield for that year states, his family was made up of one male between fifty and sixty, one male between twenty and thirty, one male between fifteen and twenty, two males between ten and fifteen, one male between five and ten; one female between fifty and sixty, one female between twenty and thirty, two females between ten and fifteen. Taking this additional record we can narrow still further the period in which he must have been born; that is, sometime between 1775 (as determined by the 1820 census) and 1780 (since he was over fifty in 1830)—quite different from the 1765–84 which we got from the 1810 census. The same is true in connection with the birth date of his wife.

This John Castle was still listed as the head of a family in Fairfield in 1840, the family then consisting of one male between sixty and seventy, one female between sixty and seventy, one female between thirty and forty, and one female between twenty and thirty. It is obvious that all the boys have married and established homes of their own or have moved away or are working somewhere and that the girls have all married except two who are staying at home with the "old folks." Living in the same neighborhood we find Stanley Castle as the head of a family consisting of two males between twenty and thirty, one male under five, two females between twenty and thirty, and one female between fifteen and twenty. From this record and the proximity of the two families, we can assume that Stanley was one of the sons of John Castle, perhaps born about 1810, that he had married some time between 1835 and 1840, as he had a son under five, and possibly that he was working the original farm (his parents having perhaps moved to a smaller house up the road, let us say) or had bought himself a farm near his father's. Possibly the male of his own age in the census was one of his brothers; and possibly the extra females were his sisters, or those of his wife.

Now, using only the data which we have obtained from the successive censuses of Fairfield, Vt., we can construct a tentative account of John Castle (I should note that no person of the name of Castle appears in the 1850 census of Fairfield), something like this:

John Castle was born between 1775 and 1780; he was living in 1840. He married about 1800, and settled in Fairfield, Vt., before 1810. He appears as a head of a family there in the United States censuses of 1810 to 1840 inclusive.

He had children:

   i. A daughter, b. *ca.* 1800–4 (under 10 in 1810; 16–26 in 1820; 20–30 in 1830).

   ii. A son, b. *ca.* 1804–10 (under 10 in 1810; 10–16 in 1820; 20–30 in 1830).

  iii. A daughter, b. *ca.* 1804–10 (under 10 in 1810; 10–16 in 1820); married or died before 1830, when she was no longer listed in her father's family.

  iv. A son, b. *ca.* 1804–10 (under 10 in 1810; 10–16 in 1820); away or dead in 1830, when he was no longer listed in his father's family.

   v. A son, b. *ca.* 1810–15 (under 10 in 1820; 15–20 in 1830); perhaps the Stanley Castle of the 1840 census.

  vi. A son, b. *ca.* 1815–20 (under 10 in 1820; 10–15 in 1830).

 vii. A son, b. *ca.* 1815–20 (under 10 in 1820; 10–15 in 1830).

viii. A daughter, b. *ca.* 1815–20 (under 10 in 1820; 10–15 in 1830).

  ix. A daughter, b. *ca.* 1815–20 (under 10 in 1820; 10–15 in 1830).

   x. A son, b. *ca.* 1820 (probably the 3d male under 10 in 1820; 5–10 in 1830).

You will have noticed that only the head of the family is named in these first five censuses, 1790 to 1840, although the classification of the members of the family by age had been extended and was much more close than in the first census. Undoubtedly this increase in the number of classes within the family was due to the government's growing interest in education and the desire to ascertain how many children of school age there were in the United States. The military interest, shown in the first census, was still there, but by 1840 men of military age were more closely classified than they had been in 1790.

Beginning with the census of 1850 each individual member of the family or household was listed by name. The age in years, the occupation, the place of birth (that is, the state or the country), and the value of the real estate of each was given. Thus, for the first time it was possible, in 1850, to determine from the census records the nationalities making up the population of the United States. From the viewpoint of the genealogist, this census

is very valuable because it does list each member of the
family by name and gives the age and place of birth of
each. Let us take a typical record from the 1850 census
of Center Township, Lake County, Ind.:

David Hungerford, aged	46, farmer, born in	Conn.
Eunice	"	"	44	"	"	N.Y.
Esther	"	"	18	"	"	Ohio
Marian	"	"	14	"	"	"
Busan D.	" (male) "	12	"	"	"
Freeman G.	"	"	10	"	"	"
Mary A.	"	"	5	"	"	Mich.
Hannah A.	"	"	2	"	"	Ind.

From this record we get the following story about the
family: David Hungerford was born in Connecticut
about 1803-4; probably he met his wife, Eunice, somewhere in Ohio and married her there about 1830; their
first four children were born in Ohio, and then, between
1840 and 1844, they moved to Michigan where they lived
but a short time; about 1846-47 they moved, probably to
Center Township, Lake County, Ind., where they were
living in the summer of 1850. It looks as though they
might have lost a child between Esther and Marian, and
another between Freeman G. and Mary A. It happens
that after obtaining the census record, I found a record
of his family, which proved the suppositions I had made,
supplied the names of the two children who died, and
gave the further information that David Hungerford removed to Oakland, Ia., and died there in 1855.

The records of all the federal censuses from 1800 to
1880, inclusive, may be consulted in the National Archives in Washington; they are also available on microfilm. You can purchase the reel of film which covers the
area in which your ancestors lived (see the note at the
end of Appendix C); but be sure you have a reading
machine which will enable you to enlarge the microfilm
copy and project it upon a surface from which you can
read it. The larger libraries have such reading machines,
and those with genealogical collections have some of the
microfilm copies, perhaps all of them. The census records
since 1890 (the 1890 schedules were burned up in a fire)

are available in the Kansas depository of the Bureau of the Census but may be used only under certain conditions, for the contents are still considered confidential. Write to the National Archives and Records Service, General Services Administration, Washington, D.C. 20408, for the earlier records. For the later ones, ask the Bureau of the Census, United States Department of Commerce, Pittsburg, Kansas 66762, for the "Application for Search of Census Records"; it lists the regulations governing their use and tells you how to obtain copies.

You should not overlook the census records as a source of information in digging for ancestors. Although those who "took" the censuses (that is, the "enumerators") were human beings and liable to error, and sometimes the person who answered the questions didn't know or didn't remember correctly, the records given in the census schedules are valuable and furnish important data which can generally be checked against other documents, such as a Bible record. In using census records, or in having them searched, try to get your ancestor pinned down to a definite locality if you possibly can. It is easier to search the records for Allegany County, New York, in 1850, even though the schedule runs to more than 700 pages, than it is to search those for the entire western end of New York State; and it saves a great deal of time if you know that your man lived in Granger township!

There are many other types of records in Washington which will be of use to you in your search for ancestors. For instance, there is a great mass of land records; there are petitions to Congress for "relief" for one reason or another (many of these are noted in the "Documents Index," which indexes the documents that have been printed; any reference librarian can show you how to use it); and there are pension records, discussed at length in the next chapter.

There is in Washington a great building devoted to the National Archives. Here, where they can be properly housed, listed, cared for, and made available to the public, the older records from the various departments, bureaus, and offices of the national government have been concentrated. The use of these records has been greatly facilitated by the introduction of modern methods of arranging them, and by the many lists, calendars, and catalogues compiled by the staff; and copying is made much easier by the use of photographic processes of one sort or another. You should write to the National Archives and Records Service, General Services Administration, Washington, D.C. 20408, for information regarding what records are available for use and whether or not your question can be answered by this office. Extensive research is generally turned over to a research worker whom you select and pay. *Genealogical Records in the National Archives* (General Information Leaflet, Number 5), obtainable free, is a twelve-page description of records of value to the ancestor hunter to be found in the archives. In fact the General Services Administration has a kit which it will send free of charge. It includes the leaflet, forms to be filled out, and prices for photocopies of certain records. There is also a more extensive (114 pages) *Guide to Genealogical Records in the National Archives*, by Meredith B. Colket, Jr., and Frank E. Bridgers. This is on sale by the Superintendent of Documents, U.S. Government Printing Office, Washington, D.C. 20402, for 65 cents. As you get into genealogical research you will probably want your own desk copy of this valuable guide to public records.

CHAPTER ELEVEN

How to Be a D.A.R.

SINCE 1890 when the Daughters of the American Revolution was organized more digging for ancestors has probably resulted from the desire to belong to this organization than has come about through any other impetus. This society, together with others in which membership is based upon lineage, is directly responsible for much of the widespread interest in the preservation of records of genealogical value. More than 200,000 lineages have been filed and preserved in the D.A.R. archives in Memorial Continental Hall in Washington, showing the descent of the members of the society from one or more patriots who served in the Revolutionary War between 1775 and 1783, or, in some cases, from women such as Molly Pitcher or from civil officers who rendered service to the cause of the Revolution. Each year hundreds of additional pedigrees are submitted, approved, and placed on file.

In the early days of the society it was comparatively simple to submit a pedigree and secure membership on the basis of it, once the invitation to become a member had been received. But, as the study of genealogy has become more and more a historical science and genealogists both professional and amateur have become more and more careful about the authenticity of any pedigree and the proof in support of it, the D.A.R. officials have been scrutinizing the pedigrees of their prospective members more and more closely, until now it is necessary to have ample proof of an authentic descent from a bona fide patriot of the Revolution. In fact the proof of this descent must be as thorough as that required to prove a claim to an estate in a court of law. Moreover, now the location of the patriot's grave must be known.

As an example of the laxity with which the older members of the D.A.R. compiled their pedigrees, let me cite one extreme case which always amuses me. A certain lady, prominent in her own city until the time of her death, became a member of her local chapter of the D.A.R. many, many years ago, at the time when the chapter was organized. Her papers, as submitted and approved, were based on the service of one Hezekiah Royce (or Rice, as the name was spelled in them), and in the course of time this pedigree was printed in the *Lineage Books* of the society. Now it happens that there were two Hezekiah Royces, one of whom was a notorious Tory and the other, his son, a brave young man who marched to the defense of Bennington in 1777. The lady's ancestor was actually the Tory, not the son, although she never knew that fact and, I believe, was at one time regent of her chapter! I suspect that that old Tory has had many a quiet chuckle over the matter—if Tories were ever permitted to enter the land of heavenly bliss and can witness the antics of their descendants.

Such a thing could not happen today, because the staff of competent and experienced genealogists who examine and pass upon the pedigrees submitted as the basis of membership would demand more proof than my old acquaintance supplied with her application. Papers must be accompanied by affidavits, certified copies of Bible records, and exact references to the sources of all data for each generation in the pedigree. In the case of doubt concerning the authenticity of any point or connecting link in the pedigree, the registrar general of the National Society will demand more proof, and further evidence must be found before the papers are approved and the candidate is admitted to membership. This tightening of the requirements has had its influence on the development of accurate genealogy and is very commendable.

In addition to service in the army and navy during the Revolutionary War, 1775–83, membership in the Daughters of the American Revolution may be based upon the following services, as outlined by the registrar general of the National Society:

a. Civil office during the Revolutionary War period, 1775–83.
b. Committee service six months before the Battle of Point Pleasant, 10 October 1774.
c. Community service such as: Tax collector, Justice of peace, Selectman, or other town officer, Hog reave, Deer keeper, Fence viewer, Surveyor of highways, Boundary commissioner, and so forth, 1775–83.
d. Boston Tea Party; Aid to Boston, 1774; Danbury raid; Galvez expedition; Cherokee expedition; ministers who preached patriotic sermons and encouraged patriotic service.
e. Women as patriots, nurses, and so forth.
f. Quakers and others who, though opposed to war, assisted in caring for sick and wounded.
g. Defenders of forts and frontiers; Rangers; Defenders of Bryan Station, Ky.; King's Mountain men; Signers of Mecklenburg Declaration, 1775; Albermarle, Va., declaration.
h. British list of prisoners on board British ship "Jersey" and other prison ships.
i. Munition makers and gun-smiths.
j. Signers of Association Tests and Oaths of Allegiance, and so forth.
k. Battle of Alamance, 1771, providing they remained loyal.
l. Signers of nonimportation agreement, 1765–70.
m. "Cornet," or banner carrier.

And, of course, descent from a signer of the Declaration of Independence.

In some cases a man in Revolutionary times was unable to go into actual service himself because of his age, infirmities, or some other reason, and found and paid a substitute to go in his place. In this event the man's patriotic intent is accepted as a service and his descendants are eligible for membership. One such case is unusually interesting. Thomas Lawton was born in Taunton, Mass., about 1731. He saw service in the French and Indian Wars, and later was called to serve in the Revolution. As he was unable to go, his eldest son, Nathaniel, a lad of sixteen, went in his place, and was soon killed at the battle of White Plains, 28 October 1776. Thus this young lad's unselfish service has made it possible for the descendants of his seven brothers and sisters to claim membership in the D.A.R. (For the story of this boy's service see Hemenway's *Vermont Historical Gazetteer,* Vol. 5, Pt. 2, p. 61.)

Once your preliminary application (which is required in some local chapters) has been approved by the local chapter—after, of course, you have received your invitation to become a member of that specific chapter of the society, or have been invited to become a member-at-large of the National Society—you will have to fill out and submit through the local chapter a pedigree blank on which there are spaces for full data concerning the birth, marriage, and death of each individual in your direct descent from the soldier (or other person) on whose service you are basing your right to membership. At least two of the three vital dates (that is, of birth, marriage, and death) for each must be given, and the evidence of the probable date of the third. For instance, let us suppose that you have from the town records the dates of birth and marriage of your great-grandfather, John Jones, son of Henry Jones, who served in the Revolution, but you cannot determine the date of his death, either from official vital records, from church records, or from his gravestone, which you have been unable to find. But you have seen a deed of land transfer which he signed ten years after your grandmother, his daughter, was born. Therefore you can enter in the space on the pedigree form allotted to his death record this fact: "Living 10 April 1838, when he signed a deed." A missing marriage date is more serious, but, even though the actual date of marriage cannot be found, evidence of the marriage can generally be produced either in the form of the signatures to a deed in which the ancestor conveyed land jointly with his wife, or from tombstones standing side by side and bearing evidence of the marriage, such as, "Hannah, wife of John Jones, died November 4th, 1839, in her 50th year," or from an obituary notice in some old newspaper, or any one of several other evidences. When all other evidence is lacking, the registrar general will accept a complete list of the children, with dates of birth, as evidence that there was a legal marriage.

In working out your descent from a Revolutionary soldier or a person who rendered any of the services listed above, you proceed as I have indicated in the preceding chapters, building up your pedigree from family records, town and church records, wills and administrations of estates, cemetery inscriptions, and printed books, such as genealogies, town histories, census records, and printed vital records. When you have worked out your line, or lines, back to the period of the Revolutionary War, you must find the service record of one or another of the ancestors who were then living, as the basis for your claim to membership in the D.A.R.

Sometimes this is an easy matter, but in other cases it is extremely difficult, for you must positively identify your ancestor as the man who rendered the service which you have found under his name in the many lists of Revolutionary soldiers. These lists have been carefully compiled from old muster rolls, pay rolls, and other records. Most of the thirteen original states, and Vermont, the fourteenth state, have published lists of their Revolutionary soldiers (see Appendix D for a bibliography of the more important books containing lists of such soldiers). Sometimes, even though your ancestor may have had as unusual and uncommon a name as Hezekiah Royce, you may find that there were several men of the same name serving from the same state or general locality. Then you must prove which one was your ancestor. Sometimes there were even two or more men of the same name living in the same community at the time of the war, one of them serving and the others not serving. In that event, you must find absolute proof of the service of your progenitor and must positively eliminate the others.

A source of great aid in identifying and proving the service of a Revolutionary soldier is the collection of pension records at the National Archives in Washington. The pension system originated in the provision made by the Continental Congress in the early days of the Revo-

lution that all officers who should serve for the duration
of the war would be entitled to receive half pay for
seven years after the war was over. In 1785, Congress
recommended to the several states that they make provision for pensioning the invalid veterans of the war. In
1808 the federal government assumed these pension obli-
gations from the several states. This provided only for
persons disabled in the service. Ten years later, in 1818,
Congress passed an act granting pensions to all who had
served nine months or more in the Revolutionary army
and were in straitened circumstances. This act was revised from time to time, and in 1836 a new act was
passed providing pensions for the widows of Revolutionary soldiers. This act was in turn revised until all
such widows, regardless of when they had married Revolutionary soldiers, were entitled to such a pension. It is
interesting to note that in 1868, when all Revolutionary
soldiers were dead, there were 888 widows of such soldiers still receiving pensions. There were thirteen in
1893!

When you have found out that your ancestor served
in the Revolution, you should learn whether or not he
ever had a pension. In 1966 the National Genealogical
Society published *An Index of Revolutionary War Pension Applications,* which is available in most of the larger
genealogical libraries. Or you can write to the National
Archives and Records Service, General Services Administration, Washington, D.C. 20408, and ask for forms on
which to apply for a Revolutionary War veteran's pension record. To fill out this form when it arrives you will
need the record of his service as you have found it in the
Revolutionary rolls or some other source, and other data
for his identification such as the year of his birth or
death, the locality in which he lived at the time of service, and that in which you think he lived when he
claimed a pension.

To secure a pension, an ex-soldier of the Revolution
had to submit to the authorities in Washington proof of
his service and his eligibility for a pension. Consequently,
the papers which he submitted to the pension bureau
contained statements, signed and sworn to, that he had
served in a specified organization and had taken part in

certain expeditions, campaigns, battles, or marches, and that he was identical with the soldier named in the rolls of the company or companies in which he claimed to have served. Moreover, he had to prove that he was "indigent" and needed assistance. Therefore, he had to file not only his own sworn statement, but also affidavits from other soldiers who served with him or knew of his service, and affidavits certifying his financial condition at the time of the claim. In some cases these papers were unusually full and contained statements regarding birth and parentage, marriage, and migrations from place to place. Sometimes the information which they supply is disappointingly meager. If the claimant was a widow to the soldier, she had to submit evidence of her marriage to the soldier on whose service she was basing her claim and, in many cases, a list of the children she had borne to him. Thus, among the pension papers is frequently found a transcript of the Bible record of the family of the soldier, the original of which may have been lost or destroyed.

Let us take a typical pension case, that of John Benjamin Mitchell, who served in the Revolution while living in Connecticut, and died in Fairfield, Vt. We find on his gravestone the data: "John B. Mitchell, died Sept. 9, 1842, in his 82nd yr. A Revolutionary Soldier." His descendants are fortunate in that they do not have to search to find out *if* he served—his gravestone states it—so there is just the actual record of service to find. From the list of pensioners appended to the 1840 census we find that he was receiving a pension at that time. So we write to the National Archives in Washington, asking for the pension record, and get the following reply:

The data furnished below were obtained from the papers on file in pension claim, W. 15,693, based upon the Revolutionary War Service of John Benjamin Mitchel or Mitchell.

The date and place of his birth and the names of his parents are not given.

John Benjamin Mitchel enlisted at Newtown, Connecticut, July 21, 1777 and served as a private in Captain Albert Chapman's company in Colonel Heman Swift's Connecticut regiment, he was in the battle of Germantown, and was shot through the leg at the battle of Monmouth, and was discharged in June, 1783.

John Benjamin Mitchel was allowed pension on his application executed April 1, 1818, then aged fifty-eight years and living in Fairfield, Franklin County, Vermont.

He married October 30, 1783 in Fairfield County, Connecticut, Jemima Sunderland. He died September 9, 1842.

His widow, Jemima Mitchel, was allowed pension on her application executed September 5, 1844, then aged eighty-four years and living in Fairfield, Franklin County, Vermont.

Their children mentioned in the claim—Lydia Mitchel aged in 1820 twenty years, and Truman Mitchel in 1844 aged sixty years and a resident of St. Albans, Vermont.

On having a private searcher in Washington abstract the papers accompanying John B. Mitchell's pension claim, we get the additional information that James Hawley, of Sheldon, Vt., knew John B. Mitchell from infancy, a possible clue to the birthplace of Mitchell, if we can find out where Hawley came from. Thomas Northrop, in his affidavit made in 1818, stated that he had known Mitchell about forty years, knew of his service, and saw him when he returned from the war: another clue to his residence before he settled in Fairfield. In September 1844, Jemima Mitchell of Fairfield, Vt., claimed a widow's pension and stated that she was then eighty-four years old, that she had married John Benjamin Mitchell in September or October 1783, and that he had died 9 September 1842. At the same time, Truman Mitchell, aged sixty, stated that he was a son of J. B. and Jemima Mitchell. On 14 October 1844 C. N. Seymour, pastor of the Congregational church of Huntington, Conn., stated that the church records contained the following: "October 30, 1783, married John Benjamin Mitchell to Jemima Sunderland." The Reverend David Ely was pastor at that time. On 18 September 1848 Jemima Mitchell, aged eighty-eight, made a claim for additional pension under the act of 2 February 1848.

This abstract of the accompanying papers has given us a definite statement of the exact place of his marriage —Huntington, Conn.—and two clues to places of residence, in addition to the place from which he enlisted.

These clues will help us to trace his ancestry, if we want to do so.

Altogether, the papers present bona fide evidence that John B. Mitchell, whose grave we found in Fairfield, Vt., was a Revolutionary soldier and that his female descendants have a basis for membership in the Daughters of the American Revolution. Incidentally, in an affidavit submitted by John B. Mitchell in connection with the pension claim of Jedediah Sherwood, another Revolutionary soldier of Fairfield, he stated that he (Mitchell) served in Colonel Swift's regiment and that he had a brother in Colonel Sheldon's regiment of Light Dragoons, thus becoming acquainted with others in that regiment, among them Jedediah Sherwood. Unfortunately, there is no index to these affidavits, so it is impossible to get at the data in them easily. One stumbles upon them only by accident, as I stumbled upon this affidavit of Mitchell when I had the pension papers of Sherwood abstracted. I do not doubt that there are innumerable evidences of Revolutionary service buried in these affidavits. Many of the soldiers who made them never claimed a pension for themselves, and the identity of many of them can probably be proven in no other way. Consequently, I hope that some day either Congress or some private organization interested in preserving such records and making them accessible in print will provide an appropriation for printing an index to the pension papers and accompanying affidavits on file in Washington. It would be of inestimable service to all genealogists and to the thousands of people who like to dig for ancestors. As an example, this affidavit made by John B. Mitchell mentions a brother in Colonel Sheldon's regiment. The roll of that regiment will furnish this brother's name, which will help in identifying the parents of John B. Mitchell.

The pension records of the soldiers who served in the War of 1812 may be of assistance to you in proving your descent from a Revolutionary soldier, for they, too, frequently contain evidences of birth and marriages, and sometimes of parentage. Incidentally, although they are of slight value in connection with Revolutionary service, there are on file in Washington pension records for the soldiers of the subsequent wars: the Mexican War, the Civil War, and so forth.

Another source of information regarding Revolutionary soldiers (and those who served in subsequent wars) is the Defense Department in Washington. Frequently that department has records of service for men who never lived to claim a pension, or for other reasons did not receive pensions. Likewise in the offices of the adjutants general of the various states, especially the thirteen original states and Vermont, there are records which are valuable in proving the service of an ancestor. Letters to these officials will frequently produce the evidence for which you are searching.

Many years ago, the National Society of the Daughters of the American Revolution began to publish *Lineage Books* containing an abstract of the pedigrees of their members. A thousand lineages are included in each of the 166 volumes which have been published, thus making accessible in print a great mass of valuable data which would otherwise be buried in Memorial Continental Hall and the archives of the hundreds of chapters of the D.A.R. Each volume has an index to the Revolutionary ancestors, called the "Roll of Honor," and an index of the "Daughters" whose pedigrees are contained in that volume. Cumulative indexes of the ancestors in Vols. 1–40, 41–80, 81–120, and 121–60 have been published. These save a great deal of time in hunting a soldier ancestor.

In 1966, the National Society of the Daughters of the American Revolution published the *DAR Patriot Index* which "contains the names of Revolutionary Patriots, both men and women whose service (between 1774–1783) and identity have been established by the National Society . . . from its organization in October 1890 through the June 1966 meeting of the National Board of Management: over 105,000 names." A supplement was published in 1971. This gives the name, dates, and pension number, if any, of each patriot on whose service membership applications have been based and were approved. If you find your ancestor's name in the list (remember, the *Index* uses the generally accepted spelling of the surname, so do not expect to find *Chezem* under *Che*; look under *Chisholm*), you can then obtain a photocopy of

the application of another descendant of that patriot
(provided it is not "closed" by request of the member
who filed that application) by sending your check for
$2.00 (the current fee as of 1972) and giving the follow-
ing information: (1) the date of your request (you would
be surprised to know how many people forget to put this
as well as the return address on their letters); (2) the
name of the D.A.R. member or prospective member;
(3) the chapter and location of the chapter; (4) the
name of the ancestor and page number in the *DAR
Patriot Index*; (5) the name and complete address, including zip code, of the individual to whom the copy is
to be sent, if other than the one placing the order. All of
this should be sent to the Treasurer General, National
Society of the D.A.R., 1776 D Street N.W., Washington,
D.C. 20006. I gather from these directions, which I have
copied from the *Index* itself, that an application for a
photocopy should be sent through some member of the
chapter in which you have been invited to become a
member. Frankly, I am a bit puzzled about the possibility of obtaining photocopies by a male who is not even
eligible for membership!

Many of the state societies of the D.A.R. and some
individual chapters have published books containing
data about the Revolutionary ancestors of their members.
A complete list of such books would be too lengthy to
include in this volume, but most larger libraries and
historical societies are likely to have them, and genealogists who make a specialty of Revolutionary ancestry
are familiar with them.

For many years individual chapters of the D.A.R. have
been interested in gathering and publishing records of
value in proving Revolutionary ancestry and other data
of use to genealogists and local historians. For instance
the Eunice Dennie Burr Chapter of Fairfield, Conn.,
compiled, under the direction and editorship of Donald
Lines Jacobus (a thoroughly reliable and competent genealogist), the *History and Genealogy of the Families of
Old Fairfield, Connecticut*. In this set the first two volumes contain the genealogies of the families settled in
Fairfield before the Revolutionary War, and the third
volume contains abstracts of the pension papers of all

Revolutionary soldiers known to be connected with that town. Many other local histories, such as this, contain lists of Revolutionary soldiers, of such soldiers as are buried in the town in which the chapter is functioning, abstracts of wills of such soldiers, transcripts of church records, histories of specific battles, and even general local histories.

During the last few years the National Society, through its Genealogical Records Committee, has encouraged each state society to make a special effort to gather unprinted records and preserve them. Typewritten copies of such records are made, and one copy is deposited in Memorial Continental Hall in Washington. In many of the states, another copy is deposited in the most prominent or accessible library in the state collecting genealogical material, where it is bound and ready for use. There are, for instance, several such volumes deposited in the State Historical Society library in Montpelier, Vt., containing records collected by the Vermont Society of the D.A.R. The Massachusetts Society is making a fine effort to copy and preserve the inscriptions in all the cemeteries in that state, particularly the old, forgotten graveyards. The Michigan Society has been sponsoring a state-wide federal relief project to copy the early vital records of the state and file them in the State Library in Lansing (records since 1870 are on file in the Health Department there).

In 1892 the National Society of the D.A.R. began publishing a magazine devoted to its interests, now known, after several changes of title, as the *Daughters of the American Revolution Magazine*. Almost every number has in it material of general interest to the ancestor hunter: short biographical sketches of Revolutionary soldiers; data about them in records of dedications of memorials to them; accounts of events in the Revolutionary War; many transcripts of marriage records from different localities; church records; indexes of obituary notices in local newspapers; abstracts of wills and administrations of estates; and other similar records. The index of each volume of this magazine is published separately and is available upon request at the close of the year.

In 1958 the National Society of the D.A.R. (1776 D

Street N.W., Washington, D.C. 20006) published a pamphlet which the prospective member, if she wants to work out her lineage herself rather than hire it done, or anyone else really interested in hunting ancestors, should get and study. It is called *Is That Lineage Right?* The subtitle states that it is "a training manual for the examiner of lineage papers, with helpful hints for the beginner in genealogical research." Part I, "Verification," includes "Types of Evidence and Their Value," "Suggestions for Checking Statement of Facts," "Printed Material as Evidence," "Vexatious Problems" like marriage records; Part II, "Aids to Verification," is a concise discussion of census records, pension and bounty land records, vital records, and the use of maps. There is also a short bibliography of carefully selected books, periodicals, and articles, particularly those covering individual states and regions. There are four appendixes; two are especially noteworthy: B. "Glossary of Abbreviations and Selected Terms," and D. "Ancestral Requirements for Membership in Various Societies." Twenty-two hereditary and patriotic societies are listed and their addresses given. This model handbook was prepared by Dr. Jean Stephenson, chairman of the Genealogical Records Committee of the National Society of the D.A.R. and Fellow of the American Society of Genealogists. Dr. Stephenson has done an exemplary piece of work in condensing into fifty-nine pages so much valuable advice and factual information. It is the best brief manual of genealogy with which I am acquainted.

CHAPTER TWELVE

How to Arrange a Genealogy

Now THAT you have gathered together a mass of notes on your ancestors, you will want to arrange them in some orderly fashion, especially if you propose to print or publish them in some way. You will probably plan to preserve what you have dug out of the various original records and hand it on to your children, your nephews, nieces, cousins, aunts, and uncles. In distributing copies of your genealogy, keep in mind the help you have had from the printed books and genealogies at your favorite library, and deposit a copy of it there and perhaps in one or two other genealogical collections, for others to use.

In using genealogies, especially those found in the *New England Historical and Genealogical Register,* you have undoubtedly noted the string of names, each with a superior number attached to it, printed in italic type and enclosed in parentheses, following the name of the head of the family. This is an abbreviated way of showing a descent in the successive generations from the emigrant ancestor or the progenitor of the family, the superior figure indicating the number of the generation, thus (*James*[4] *John*[3] *Henry*[2] *John*[1]). This, interpreted, means that James was of the fourth generation and a son of John the third generation, who was a son of Henry of the second generation, this Henry being a son of John the emigrant, or the progenitor of the family.

Because of this custom of using superior figures to indicate the generations, which has developed through long usage, it is unwise and confusing to use the same device in a genealogy for reference to footnotes or authorities, in the way such numbers are used in histories and other works. For this purpose it is better to use letters of the alphabet, or figures enclosed in parentheses, thus (1), or the customary symbols (*, †, ‡, §, ||, ¶, etc.).

You should write first the account of the progenitor (or emigrant ancestor) of the family whose genealogy you have been preparing. In the first paragraph should be given the dates of his birth and death, his parentage (if known), and the authorities for these statements. Incidentally, if only one fact is taken from some authority, that source should be cited immediately following the information gained from it; if more than one fact comes from that authority, the reference may be cited at the end of your account of that generation and referred to by a superior letter or figure in parentheses.

The next paragraph should contain the record of the progenitor's marriage, giving the place and date if known (or, if not known, the approximate date and the reasons supporting it), the bride's full name and her parentage, as well as the dates of her birth and death. If she was a widow, the name of her first husband should be given; and if she married a second or a third time, the name or names of her successive husbands should be noted—this is all a part of her history. Interesting details of her life and accomplishments can be reserved for a later paragraph.

If this progenitor had two or more wives, I prefer to give a separate paragraph to each marriage and the vital details about each wife. It sets the successive marriages apart in the text and enables anyone using the genealogy to find quickly the data for which he is searching.

Following the marriage paragraph (or paragraphs) should come the account of the life, activities, and accomplishments of the head of the family—his military service, the offices which he held in civil life, the migrations which he made, and all such details as will help you or your prospective reader to paint a picture of him.

In a paragraph by itself should be given an abstract of his will and that of his wife (or widow) if she made one. In abstracting a will you should note the relationship of the heirs to the testator, as mentioned in it, and any

other interesting details which you think should be noticed. The date of the will and the date of probate should
always be given. In the absence of a will, any details
gleaned from the administration of the estate should be
given, as well as abstracts of any deeds or conveyances
which contain genealogical evidence.

Then, beginning a final paragraph with some such
phrase as "The children of . . . and . . . (. . .) . . ." or
simply the word "Children" or "Issue," you should list in
columnar form all the children of this progenitor or head
of a family. I like to follow the "Register form," as the
style used in the *New England Historical and Genealogical Register* is called, using small Roman numerals to
indicate the order of birth (even if, in the absence of
specific evidence, you have had to arrange them hypo-
thetically), and reserving the Arabic numerals for the
child (or, in the case of a comprehensive genealogy of
all the descendants of the progenitor, the children)
whose line is carried on.

Following the account of the children, you can list the
general references used in building up the history of this
generation of the family. In giving references to books
you should always use the author's name and the title of
the book as given on its title page, rather than the "binder's title," or title from the back of the bound volume
(binder's titles may vary in different libraries, but the
title page is always the same wherever you use the
book). If there is a date of publication on the title page,
it should be cited in parentheses following the title of the
book; if there is no date on the title page, use the copy-
right date given on the back of the title page, or the date
at the end of the preface. Any of these dates not only
serves to identify the edition of the book that you have
used, but indicates the approximate time when the record you abstract from that book was obtained by its
author.

Now let us see what this looks like in printed form.
I am writing up, as an example, an imaginary family in
which all names, places of residence, and other data are
fictitious. I give the "records" of two generations and two
families only, but my use of Arabic numerals indicates

that this is a comprehensive genealogy of all John Jones's descendants.

The Descendants of John Jones

GENERATION I

1. JOHN JONES was born, probably in England, about 1750–51; he died in Pollock, Blank County, N.Y., 23 April 1833, aged 83 years, according to his gravestone in the Pine Grove Cemetery there. His parentage is unknown, but it has been said that he was the younger son of a prominent English family and that he came to America as an officer in the British Army during the Revolution. Convinced of the righteousness of the American cause, he resigned his commission, assumed the name of Jones, and enlisted in the Continental Army. He never disclosed his real name, and no evidence of it has been found. There can be little doubt of his English origin, for he was referred to as "John the Englishman" in the Pollock Town Records, apparently to distinguish him from another John Jones living in Pollock at that time [Pollock Town Records, Book B, p. 26].

He married, 1 May 1783, at Allen, Mass., Mary Smith, daughter of James and Mary (Hancock) Smith. She was born in Allen, 3 August 1760; she died in Pollock, N.Y., 29 January 1851, and was buried beside her husband in the Pine Grove Cemetery.

John Jones served in the Massachusetts Line in the Revolutionary War from 1780 to 1783. He claimed a pension in 1820. His pension record in Washington shows his service, but gives no indication of his birth or parentage. His widow received a pension, and her papers give the place and date of their marriage and contain a transcript of the Bible records of their children. (The Bible appears to be lost.)

After his marriage, John Jones and his wife lived in Allen, Mass., for two or three years. About 1786 they removed to New York state, and were living in Pollock by 1790 [U.S. census, 1790, New York, p. 221]. He was a miller, and is said to have established the first mill in Pollock. He held several town offices, and was a member of the Congregational Church in Pollock.

His wife, Mary, is said to have been a woman of considerable ability as a nurse. The obituary notice of her in the Pollock *Messenger*, 31 January 1851, comments on her kindliness and notes the great esteem in which she was held by the community.

John Jones's will was dated 30 March 1833, and probated 6 July 1833. He mentioned his wife Mary, eldest surviving son Henry, sons Eugene, George W. (if he is found within two years), and Jonas; and his daughters Mary Martin and Almira Martin (deceased) and her son John Jones Martin. [Surrogate court records, Blank County, N.Y., Book D, pp. 195–201.]

Issue:

    i. John, Jr., b. in Allen, Mass., 21 June 1784; d. 22 June 1784.

    ii. Mary, b. in Allen, Mass., 15 June 1785; d. young.

2. iii. Henry, b. in New York, 5 July 1787.

3. iv. James Smith, b. 28 June 1789; removed to Michigan.

4. v. Mary, b. in Pollock, N.Y., 1 July 1791; mar. Henry Martin.

5. vi. Almira, b. in Pollock, N.Y., 6 September 1793; mar. John Martin.

    vii. Eugene, b. 15 September 1795; d. unmar. 29 March 1850.

    viii. George Washington, b. 1 September 1797; disappeared in the West before 1833.

    ix. John (twin), b. 6 April 1800; d. 15 April 1800.

6. x. Jonas (twin), b. 6 April 1800.

References:

Biographical sketch of John Jones in William Johnson's *History of Blank County, N.Y.* (1879), pp. 345–46.

Vital Records of Allen, Massachusetts, to 1850 (1910), p. 37.

Pension record of Jones Jones, No. W. 56,666, Washington, D.C.

Surrogate Court Records, Blank County, N.Y., Book D, pp. 195–201.

Inscriptions, Pine Grove Cemetery, Pollock, N.Y.

2. HENRY JONES (*John*[1]), son of John and Mary (Smith) Jones, was born, probably in Pollock, N.Y., 5 July 1787; he died in Whosset, Iowa, 31 December 1869, and was buried in the Center Cemetery, Buren, Ill., beside his wife.

He married, in Pollock, N.Y., 25 December 1810, Sarah Allen, daughter of Joseph and Sarah (Smith) Allen, and sister of his brother James's wife. Her mother is supposed to have been a sister of his mother. Sarah Allen was born in Allen, Mass., 25 December 1790; she died in Buren, Ill., 3 June 1860, and was buried in the Center Cemetery there.

Henry Jones served in the War of 1812 and was present at the Battle of Lake Erie. For this service he received a pension in 1858, which was continued until his death. [Pension records, Washington, D.C.]

As the western country was opened up in the years following the War of 1812, he became interested, and finally moved to Buren, Black County, Ill., about 1840. He lived there until the death of his wife, and then went to Iowa to live with his son, John.

In his will, dated 16 March 1867 and proved 5 January 1870, he mentioned his deceased wife Sarah, and expressed a desire to be buried beside her. He named also his sons John, Henry, George, and Joseph; his daughter Sarah Martin; his grandchildren Henry and Sarah Griffith, children of his deceased daughter Mary; and his grandson James, son of his son John.

Issue (all born in Pollock, N.Y.):

7.   i. Mary, b. 10 October 1811; d. 16 June 1849; mar. Jonathan Griffith.
8. ii. John, b. 29 March 1815.
    iii. Henry, b. 4 April 1817; living in 1867.
9. iv. Sarah, b. 17 March 1819; mar. Joseph Martin.
    v. Hannah, b. 25 October 1821; d. 3 January 1822; bur. in Pine Grove Cemetery, Pollock, N.Y.
   vi. Jane, b. 13 October 1823; d. 6 July 1830; bur. in Pine Grove Cemetery, Pollock, N.Y.
10. vii. George Washington, b. 9 February 1826.
11. viii. Joseph, b. 29 February 1828.

References:

Bible record in possession of Mary Jones, eldest daughter of John Jones, Whosset, Iowa.

Smith, William E., *History of Blank County, Illinois* (1886), p. 801.

Vital Records of Allen, Massachusetts to 1850 (1910), p. 10.

Will of Henry Jones, Blank County Probate Office, Ill., Book 9, pp. 222–23.

If you want to write up your direct line of descent from, let us say, John Jones, you should give Arabic nu-

DESCENDANTS OF JOHN JONES, OF POLLOCK, N.Y.

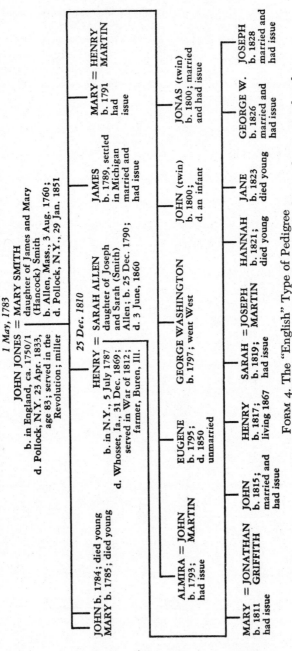

FORM 4. The "English" Type of Pedigree

This is a type of graphic pedigree much used by English genealogists but somewhat less common in America. It presents in greatly condensed form the data given in my genealogy of the hypothetical Jones family as printed on pages 133–35.

merals to that child in each successive generation from whom you descend.

Your pedigree blanks form only a skeleton of your pedigree. The complete details of each line of descent should be written up in the style I have just given. If you want to examine a fine example of this type of genealogy, one in which the ancestry of a man has been worked out in detail, look at Mary Walton Ferris's *The Dawes-Gates Ancestral Lines,* in which she worked out in elaborate detail the ancestry in all lines of Rufus Dawes and his brother, General Charles Dawes.

An excellent example of the comprehensive genealogy of the descendants of an immigrant, worked out in detail and noted for its accuracy is Donald Lines Jacobus's *Bulkeley Genealogy: Rev. Peter Bulkeley, Being an Account of His Career, His Ancestry, the Ancestry of His Two Wives, and His Relatives in England and New England, Together with a Genealogy of His Descendants through the Seventh American Generation.*

These books are models which you should study and follow in writing up the account of your family, for each has been compiled and written by an accomplished genealogist, whose ability and reputation for accurate, painstaking, documented work is well known.

CHAPTER THIRTEEN

Odds and Ends to Help Your Search

The Calendar

A STUMBLING block for many an ancestor hunter, when he attempts to check the dates of his forebears, is a mysterious discrepancy of either a few days or a year which throws out his calculation. If this does not arise, then the "double" date which he finds in some old record may cause him to wonder why those who made the contemporary record did not know whether the child was born in 1701 or 1702. If you have much experience with them, you will note that these double dates occur in the old records only in January, February, and March —never in any other months and never after 1752.

This system of double-dating arose as a result of a change made in the calendar in 1582. Before that date the so-called Julian calendar was used throughout the Christian world. It was established by Julius Caesar, hence its name. This system, which divided the year into 365 days, plus an extra day every fourth year, was officially adopted at the sitting of the Nicene Council in A.D. 325. As it became possible to measure more accurately the length of the solar year, it was found that the Julian system of measuring exceeded the solar year by eleven minutes, or twenty-four hours every 131 years, and three days every 400 years. This excess amounted to about ten days between A.D. 325 and A.D. 1582. Thus the date of the vernal equinox had been thrown back, by that time, from 21 March to 11 March and the calculations for Easter were thrown out.

In 1582 Pope Gregory XIII, then head of the Roman

Catholic Church, ordered that ten days be dropped out of the calendar, thus restoring the equinox to its accustomed date, 21 March. To prevent the recurrence of this error, he ordered further that, in every four hundred years, leap year's extra day should be omitted three times. To accomplish this in an orderly fashion it was to be omitted on centennial years of which the first two digits could not be divided by four without a remainder. Thus it was omitted in A.D. 1700, 1800, and 1900, but will not be omitted in A.D. 2000. Moreover, the decree changed the beginning of the new year from 25 March to 1 January. This system, known as the Gregorian calendar, now prevails and we are right with the sun.

Following the edict of the Pope, all Catholic countries adopted the new system of reckoning. But England, in difficulties with the Church of Rome and always reluctant to accept a new and untried idea, even though scientifically proved, refused to adopt the new calendar officially and did not adopt it until 1752, or 170 years later, when the difference between the calendar and the sun was a little more than eleven days. So in English-speaking countries (including the English colonies) and in Russia, the Julian calendar continued to prevail as the official system of counting time. Throughout that time (that is, until 1752) the new year did not begin until 25 March, and there was still a difference of eleven days between the English calendar and that used in the rest of Europe.

In spite of this difference in the official calendar, many people began to use the Gregorian system. Hence, in many of the early colonial records you will find "double dates," generally written like this: "9 March 1656/57," indicating that, while it was officially still 1656, some people considered it as 1657. Governor Winthrop dated a letter to his wife 22 March 1629; six days later he wrote another and dated it 28 March 1630.

Incidentally, in dates of the seventeenth century you will frequently find the month indicated by its number rather than its name. This was primarily because most of the months had "pagan" names and hence those names were disliked by the Puritans, and even more by the Quakers, who believe in simplicity carried to its extreme.

Since, before 1752, March was considered the first month of the year, even though the twenty-fifth was the day on which the year changed, we must interpret the old records with that in mind. Thus "13th, 2nd month, 1644"; becomes "13 April 1644"; or "3:12mo:1639" becomes "3 February 1639" (that is, 1640). Generally the day was given first and the month second, but you should always make sure by comparing the date with others in the same record, remembering that there were but twelve months and a possible thirty-one days. If you find that a date is given at 3:28:1644, you know that "3" represents the month —May; but if the record is 3:8:1644, you should try to find in the same record a date which definitely establishes the first figure as that of the month, as 4:15:1644.

In 1752, when the British government finally decided to recognize the fact that men had made a mistake in calculating the length of the solar year, and to shift into line with the other countries of Europe in the use of the calendar, Parliament passed an act by which the Gregorian system was officially adopted. It is said that there were riots in some of the rural sections of England because the act ordered that eleven days should be dropped out of the calendar following 2 September (making the next day 14 September). The people thought that the government was trying to cheat them out of eleven days of their lives! (Incidentally, the bill enacting the change was introduced in the House of Lords by the Earl of Chesterfield whose *Letters to His Son* is one of the classics of English literature.)

To cite an example of what this change meant, let us consider the birth date of George Washington. He was actually born, according to the official calendar in force at the time, 11 February 1732. But, with the change in the calendar in 1752, he changed his birthday to conform with the new calendar and thus made it 22 February in order that he could celebrate, I suppose, the exact anniversary of his birth. Therefore, to state his birth date accurately, we should write: "Born 11 February 1731, O.S. (that is, old style), or 22 February 1732, N.S. (new style)." When the genealogist attempts to correlate birth records, he should always remember this difference of eleven days and the change in the beginning of the new year. If your ancestor's gravestone states that he died "August 31, 1810, aged 81 years, 6 months, 19 days" and you figure back from that record and determine that he was born 12 February 1729, and then you find the date of his birth in the vital records of his native town as 1 February 1728, you can account for the discrepancy by this change in the calendar, for 12 February 1729 would be the "new style" of reckoning, and 1 February 1728 the "old style."

Most people do not change into new style the dates of these old records, when both of the dates (that is, those of birth and death) occurred before the change in the calendar. Even if one date is old style and one new style, it is not necessary to make the change for it can be designated by the initials "O.S." or "N.S." to indicate that you have noted any discrepancy that you have found. In the case of the "double dates" occurring between 1 January and 25 March, the year is generally designated "1640/41" or, as some of them have been printed, "164%1."

Frequently this matter of the change in the calendar will explain the birth of two children apparently within too short a period. Thus, if you have collected the data on the births of the children of a family from different sources, you can reconcile them by studying the calendar. Suppose that you find, from one source, that John and Mary Jones had a son, named Henry, born 27 March 1640, and from another record a daughter, named Hannah, born 28 February 1640. This looks very strange until you remember that the 28 February 1640 was "old style" and actually, according to modern reckoning, 28 February 1641; therefore you can figure that these two children were born eleven months apart, instead of twenty-seven days apart.

Terms of Relationship Used
in Early Records

One matter very confusing to those who begin to dig for ancestors in the early records is that of the terms used to designate relationship in ancient wills, deeds, diaries, and letters. Unless you are familiar with the variant meanings which these words had in the seventeenth century you are likely to make some serious errors.

One of the most tricky terms of this sort is "cousin." Today we think of a cousin as the son or daughter of one of our uncles or aunts, or someone more remotely related but descending from a common ancestor, and we speak of "first cousins," "cousins-german," or "own cousins" to indicate an exact degree of cousinship—that is, a son or daughter of a brother or sister of either of our parents. "Second cousin" means a grandchild of our great-uncle or great-aunt, and so forth. The child of a "first cousin" or "own cousin" is our first or own cousin once removed. But in seventeenth-century wills one frequently finds the term "cousin" applied to any relative not a brother or sister, son or daughter. Thus a man, making his will in 1650, might call his grandchild "cousin," or he might use the term to refer to a nephew, niece, uncle, aunt, or any other close relative except blood brother, sister, son, or daughter. Thus John Hubbard is called "Cousin" in the wills of both Robert Merriam and Mary Merriam of Concord in the seventeenth century. Since no records of the exact relationship have been found, we can assume merely that John Hubbard was in some way connected with Robert Merriam or his wife Mary and may have been a nephew.

"Son-in-law" and "daughter-in-law" were terms which sometimes had a different meaning in seventeenth-century records. A man was quite likely to call a stepchild (that is, child of his wife by a former marriage) "son-in-law" or "daughter-in-law" in his will.

On the other hand, "son" and "daughter" were sometimes used in that period in the sense in which we use, "son-in-law" and "daughter-in-law." You have to reason out just what was meant by the term and try to find evidence of the exact relationship.

"Brother" is another tricky term. Sometimes it meant blood brother, sometimes stepbrother, sometimes brother-in-law, and frequently "brother in the church," as it is still used in some evangelical sects. Wordy old Judge Samuel Sewall, he of the *Diary*, frequently called a man "Brother" who had no degree of relationship with him. He appears to have attended the funerals of innumerable "brothers" or "sisters" who were in no way related to him or his several successive wives. In other records, even in such serious documents as wills, the term was used to designate even the husband of a sister-in-law. In a letter, written by Thomas Hungerford of Connecticut in 1657 to Anne, wife of John Leigh, of Ipswich, Mass., he calls her "sister" and thanks her for her offer to take care of his motherless daughter, Sarah. On the basis of this letter it has been assumed that John Leigh's wife, Anne, was Thomas Hungerford's sister. There is no other evidence of the relationship, although John Leigh, in his will dated in 1671, made a bequest to this Sarah Hungerford. It seems more likely that Anne Leigh was a sister of Thomas Hungerford's first wife, whose maiden surname is unknown. Thomas Hungerford was about to marry a second wife in 1657, when this letter was written, so it is quite possible that he should send his young daughter (Sarah was born about 1654) to her mother's sister and keep with him his son, Thomas Jr. (born about 1648). Neither John Leigh, nor his widow, Anne, mentioned Thomas Hungerford's son or his daughter Hannah (by his second wife) in their wills.

"Mother" and "father" are likewise terms which did not always imply the relationship with which they are associated today. They might mean "mother-in-law" or "father-in-law" or even a stepparent acquired through the remarriage of a parent.

Frequently old records will refer to "Mrs." or "Mistriss" Sarah Jones, let us say. If you find such a title before a girl's name in a colonial marriage record, it does not mean necessarily that she was a widow or had been married before. In the seventeenth and even in the eighteenth century the title "Mistriss" (often abbreviated to "Mrs." in records) was one of social distinction as a general rule. Its use did not necessarily mean that the woman to whom it was applied was, or had been, married, as it does now. Records of the 1690's exist in which the title was given to an unmarried girl of seventeen who belonged to a family of considerable standing in the community. Sometimes the recorder used the term "Widow" if the bride had been married before and had lost her husband, although in some records you will find "Mrs." meaning widowhood. As you work with the records, you will learn to distinguish the meaning and use the title correctly.

In early colonial days in New England, "Mister" (or Mr.) was a title of respect given only to those who held important civil office or were of gentle blood before coming to Boston or Plymouth. If a man did not act in accordance with the dignity of the title "Mr." it was taken away from him, as some of the old records show. About the only title which outranked it was "Deacon." For instance, in the early records of Plymouth Colony, my ancestor was called "Mr. John Done," but after he was made a deacon he was always referred to as "Deacon John Done," thus indicating the attitude of the times toward titles.

"Goodman" and "goodwife" were titles applied to those who had the respect of their fellow colonists but who did not quite merit the titles "Mr." and "Mrs." A man who had the right to vote or conduct business in the community was entitled to be called "freeman." When a man was "admitted freeman" in a community, it indicated that he was not an indentured servant any longer (if he had been one) and was free to commit himself in trade and to vote.

The inexperienced genealogist will do well to study carefully all the available records of a family before he accepts too literally in the modern sense any of the terms expressing relationship, particularly when he finds them in old documents originally written in the seventeenth century. Inaccurately interpreted or unthinkingly accepted, they may lead you into difficulty and cause you to claim as ancestors people whose blood does not flow in your veins.

The English Origin of Emigrants to America

Another pitfall into which an inexperienced ancestor hunter is likely to tumble is that of assuming that he has determined the English connection of his family merely because he has found, in some English record, a man whose name is the same as that of his emigrant ancestor. Even in seventeenth-century England there were many people of the same name. A careful search of English records for the origin of Jehu Burr, one of the early settlers of Connecticut, has produced four men of that name, any one of whom could have been the Jehu of Connecticut. Or, to take another case, just because you know that Christopher Bannister, of Marlborough, Mass., probably came from England, you are not justified in assuming that he was identical with the Christopher Bannister who was mentioned on page 23 of the *Visitation of Lancashire in 1613* (published by the Chetham Society in 1871). That Christopher actually became the vice-chancellor of the Duchy of Lancaster, and it is extremely unlikely that he came to New England. You may, however, accept this unusual combination of names as a clue to the possible origin of your ancestor, and instigate a search of the records in Lancashire in the hope of finding evidence that your Christopher Bannister came from that county or was connected with the Bannisters of the Banke whose pedigree is recorded in the *Visitation*. Or, because I find a will in the Probate Registry of Chester in which William Done of the City of Chester mentions his son "John Done, now of London," and that will is dated 1629, I am not justified in assuming that my ancestor, John Done, who is known to have been in London before he came to Plymouth in 1630, was the son of William of Chester. It is a clue, but nothing more than that, and I must find evidence that the John mentioned in the will was identical with the John who came to Plymouth the next year. Similarity of name is not enough proof. There must be other evidence.

Browning's *Americans of Royal Descent* (especially the earlier editions of it) is full of assumptions having no more basis than this of identical names. Many of these assumptions have been proved erroneous, and none of them should be accepted without further proof. However, such is the credulity of the human race that many people blindly accept anything that they find in print, regardless of the glaring errors it contains. Let a statement be printed and intelligence seems to fly away from the reader. Another book, quite as notorious as Browning's for its errors, is David Starr Jordan's *Your Family Tree*. Dr. Jordan, himself a distinguished scientist accustomed to weighing evidence, had many assistants who used many books, including Browning's, without discrimination and copied from them long and illustrious pedigrees, which were reprinted, errors and all, in this volume. Along comes some inexperienced ancestor hunter and finds in it a "lovely" line of ancestors, descendants from kings and royal princes, all assigned a place in the pedigree without a single word of authority. "Aha, I have royal blood," he exclaims proudly, and blithely copies the supposed line, even though as a practical man of affairs he would not admit an impostor's claim to his great-uncle's estate merely on the basis of a biographical sketch printed in some old, cheap county history, written from hearsay. A pedigree which you accept as your own should be as well proved as any relationship established in a court of law.

Those of you who are interested in royal ancestry— and it is a perfectly legitimate interest to have—should read what Donald Lines Jacobus has to say on the subject in his admirable book *Genealogy as Pastime and Profession* (New Haven, 1930; reprinted with revisions, Baltimore, 1968).

The Family Coat of Arms

The use of a coat of arms in the United States is a matter of personal taste. Unless you have a coat of arms that is registered as a trademark in the Patent Office, there is no government authority which can prevent any other individual from using it. Moreover, there is no law by which you can obtain a coat of arms. Since our government does not recognize coat armor, it has become a matter of custom that we should use heraldic insignia only from personal choice, and in so using we should abide by the laws governing its use in the country in which our family originated. Therefore, since many of us who go digging for ancestors are of English origin, we should follow the English law covering the use of coats of arms. Moreover, laws or customs regarding the right to use arms vary from country to country, so the place of nativity of the progenitor has a bearing on your "right" to arms.

Heraldry is of truly ancient origin. Even in ancient Greece and Rome we find evidence that family insignia were used. By the time of the Norman Conquest of England, many individuals used such devices. As the use of armor developed and it became impossible to distinguish one man from another when the visor of his helmet was closed, it came to be the custom to wear a surcoat over the metal armor, on which were embroidered the "arms," or insignia, which the individual used to distinguish himself. This was generally identical with the insignia on the banner which his men carried and came to be known as the "coat of arms" of his family, as it was handed on from generation to generation. Gradually laws were made governing the use of coats of arms, and by the fifteenth century a definite code had been established. In the sixteenth century the College of Heralds, under whose jurisdiction the use of coat armor was placed, began a series of "visitations" of the several counties of England to determine what arms were being borne and who was entitled to them. These visitations, containing as they do thousands of pedigrees, are a source of knowledge for the genealogist as well as a record of arms. Since that time, arms have been granted by the Crown on the authority of the College of Heralds, and today you must either prove your right to bear a coat which has been confirmed by the college or pay a fee for a grant of arms.

In using a coat granted or confirmed several centuries ago, you must prove your descent from the family which originally used that coat, and establish your right to the same arms. Now, the right to bear arms descends in the male line only. Even if you assume a coat of arms without the authority of the College of Heralds, you should use only the arms which have been borne by your paternal line. A woman did not go to war in the Middle Ages and hence did not bear arms and wear coat armor. Therefore, although it is perfectly proper for you to blazon your mother's family arms in your account of her descent, you should not assume those arms as your device. According to the English law, you can quarter your father's arms with your mother's, provided she was an "heiress" and had no brothers. But I do not propose to go into the matter of quartering arms here, for it is too extensive a subject, and in some of the books to which I shall refer you it is treated more fully than I have space for treating it.

Looking up your surname in some armory, and assuming that you have a right to the coat of arms described therein, is not enough. You must prove your descent from the family to whom those arms were granted or confirmed by the College of Heralds. If you are willing to go to the expense of having those arms confirmed to you, or if you wish a new coat granted to you, you must apply to the College of Heralds in London, England, and go through the same procedure which any Englishman would go through in a similar case.

Although your name may be an unusual one, such as Hungerford, you should find proof of the connection of your immigrant ancestor with the family who bore the arms in England. In the case of the Hungerford family, we lack any evidence whatsoever of the English connection of Thomas Hungerford in Connecticut (1639), Thomas in Maryland (1641), or William in Maryland (1642). All were undoubtedly of the same blood as the English family of that name, but until their places in the English pedigrees are established, their descendants have no right (according to English law) to use the Hungerford arms as given in Burke's *General Armory*.

Because of the interest in coat armor in America, the New England Historic Genealogical Society of Boston, Mass., has a Committee on Heraldry. This committee has investigated the claims of several hundred American families to bear coat armor and has published a roll of authentic coats of arms. This is as near as we come on this side of the ocean to anything like the English College of Heralds.

An excellent book on the use of coats of arms is *The Right to Bear Arms*, which was published anonymously in England several years ago. The standard book on heraldry is *Boutell's Manual of Heraldry* (there is a revised edition, edited by C. W. Scott-Giles, published in 1954). Another good one is Francis J. Grant's *The Manual of Heraldry* (1924). Of the older armories the best known is Sir John Bernard Burke's *The General Armory of England, Scotland, Ireland, and Wales* (1878), generally referred to as *Burke's Armory*. The 1884 edition was reprinted in 1969. It is useful because it attempts to list all known coats of arms ever used in England.

A brief, interesting, and informative little book is that by Sir Anthony R. Wagner, K.C.V.O., Garter King-of-Arms, the College of Arms Heralds, London, and a Fellow of the American Society of Genealogists, *Heraldry in England* (King Penguin Books, 1946). I quote one sentence from it: "An honest pedigree, however unambitious, and a new shield [that is, grant of arms] though without pretence to nobility, may warm its owner's heart, make him hold his head higher and feel himself the heir of a great tradition" (page 24). To be aware that one is an "heir," has continuity with the past, and is, as it were, a link between that past and the future gives one a sense of belonging, of being a part of God's plan of history, however humble one's progenitors may have been. Even though an ancestor here or there in the family tree may have been licentious or profligate, a horse thief or a scoundrel, a criminal or a convict, one can always be thankful that such were exceptions in the family who, in spite of their personal propensities or uncontrolled appetites (and, in some instances, the forces of circumstances which surrounded them), failed to break the continuity of the family, however much they may appear to be abnormal growths in one of its branches. In contrast, the rest of the ancestral line stands worthy and reliable, and the descendants may take justifiable pride in the fact that they have conquered the tendencies which, for a brief space, got out of control, and have done their part to restore the family to wholesomeness.

Bound Boys and Orphans

Several have asked me what it means when one discovers a tradition, or the fact, that great-grandfather, let us say, was a "bound boy" or an "indentured servant" or was taken from an orphanage. My old, reliable *Century Dictionary* (10 vols., 1896), a useful tool for quick reference because it includes phrases and illustrative quotations as well as words, defines "bind" (in this sense) as "to indenture as an apprentice: often [used] with *out*." A son was "bound out" by his father, his widowed mother, or his guardian to give him training in some craft or trade, or, perchance, to relieve the parent from the expense of feeding and clothing him during his minority. Orphanages regularly bound out boys and girls in the same way that they might be trained to support themselves. This system of indentured apprenticeship undoubtedly had its origin in the trade guilds of the Middle Ages. During the course of the centuries various laws governing and controlling it have been enacted, but we need not go into its history here—if you are interested, read the short but excellent article in the 11th edition of the *Encyclopaedia Britannica* as an introduction and then Abbot Emerson Smith's *Colonists in Bondage: White Servitude and Convict Labor in America, 1607–1776* (1947), noting especially the bibliographical appendix, pages 397–417.

For our purpose it is sufficient to say that, from early colonial days, a boy might be "bound out" to a master, who, under the terms of the indenture (or legal agreement), had to provide him training in his craft or trade and give him board, lodging, and clothes, and perhaps pay him a stipulated sum at the end of his term. This was usually seven years or, in some instances, until the boy came of age. A farmer, lacking sufficient help, would take a boy in this way to help him with the farm work, or a girl to help his wife spin and weave and cook; a goldsmith, or printer, or paper-maker would do the same to get assistants and to train them. The boy so indentured would, in seven years, learn the craft and be able to take care of himself at the end of the contract. A widow, bereaved of her husband and left with little support, might bind out one or more of the elder children in order to provide them with a trade and at the same time relieve herself of their support.

An indentured servant was generally one who, wanting to migrate to America, the land of golden opportunities, where he thought he would have a better chance of improving his condition than he would in his native country, would sell his services (the only asset he might have) to someone by indenturing himself as a servant in return for the passage money which he had to get to the New World. By this indenture he contracted to work for the man who advanced the money for a specified number of years. Some of the passengers on the famous *Mayflower* were such servants, my own ancestor, George Soule, among them.

Some masters were exacting, severe, even cruel and inhuman in their treatment of their apprentices and "indentured servants," in fact used them like slaves; others were fair and kindly, even though they may have been strict and insistent upon full service and good workmanship; and some went further and treated their "bound boy" or girl as a member of the family.

Although it may be difficult, it is not always impossible to find the parentage of a bound boy, or an orphan. Indentures of apprenticeship were generally matters of public record, so the records of them may be found in county courthouses or other repositories such as the state archives—the custodianship of such records varies in different periods and in the several states. In some, for instance, there is an orphans' court in the county organization; in others the records may be kept in some division of the municipal government. See, for example, pages 55–58 in Rosalie Fellows Bailey's *Guide to Genealogical and Biographical Sources for New York City (Manhattan) 1783–1898* (1954) for her account of the records of orphans and apprentices in that city. Perhaps the best way to locate records of indenture or orphanage is to write to the county clerk and ask for information—failing that, try the secretary of state at the state capitol. Again, let me warn you, in writing to an official for the records of a specific individual, give him in concise form all the data which you have and especially the approximate dates, if you do not have a specific date.

To descend from a bound boy, an orphan, or an indentured servant, is nothing to be ashamed of or sensitive about. Poverty is not a disgrace nor is orphanage, whatever may have been the circumstances which brought it about. Not all children in orphanages were illegitimate or of unknown parentage, but all were wards of the state through no fault or act of their own and should be respected as human beings and treated with sympathy and understanding, if for no other reason than that they were deprived of parental affection and normal family life. Even illegitimate parentage should not be the reason for condemning the individual so born.

Illegitimate and Adopted Children

Speaking of illegitimate and adopted children: I have been asked about the treatment of such cases in a genealogy or family history. This may well become a moot point when the genealogies of many twentieth-century families are compiled, considering some attitudes now prevalent. Many illegitimate children are acknowledged by their fathers or their fathers are identified in records. In some instances they even bear the father's name. In fact, in the New England colonies, now states, an illegitimate birth was frequently recorded under the mother's name and the child given its father's surname; in some instances the birth may be recorded under both names, paternal and maternal. I have found such cases in Rhode Island records. An illegitimate child is in no way to blame for the accident of his birth, though in times past many have been stigmatized by a cruel, inhuman society. In our time, I trust, we are less censorious and more willing to accept men and women on their merits, equal in the sight of God.

Certainly in the compilation of a genealogy illegitimate or adopted children bearing the surname of the family should be given full treatment if they live to adulthood and have progeny and hence are carried forward as heads of family groups. Although adopted children usually do not have the "blood," they too bear the name and hand it down to their descendants. When the actual parentage of an adopted child is known it should be recorded in the genealogy. That is what I have advised when I have been consulted. The fact of illegitimacy or adoption can be given in a footnote, with as much detail as the compiler decides to use. When such a person is carried forward as the head of a family group, such information need not be repeated or amplified if the compiler has any qualms about it.

Where to Go to School

In recent years several courses and seminars in genealogy have been offered for those who want instruction before going further in their search for ancestors. Before taking such a course, it is well, however, to have gathered at least a few records of your progenitors, gained a little experience, and know what your problems are. In many of these, in addition to lectures, there is some type of laboratory work and you are graded, in part at least, on the way you handle a problem. The instructor may assign to you a case which will involve using the kinds of records which he has been discussing, or he may have you take one of your own problems and apply to it the principles he has given you and expect you to use the appropriate sources in your efforts to find the solution. Sometimes a problem of your own choosing in your own ancestry may be worked upon, or you are given an opportunity to discuss it with one of the instructors. This is good practice, for you have his expert guidance in your searching.

In 1950 the American University in Washington, D.C., began to sponsor an annual Institute of Genealogical Research under the able direction of Dr. Jean Stephenson and Meredith B. Colket, Jr., in cooperation with the American Society of Genealogists, the Maryland Hall of Records in Annapolis, and the National Archives and Records Service. In 1972, the National Archives and Records Service, whose resources have always been an important part of the seminar, took over the management and has continued the annual institute. It is usually held for three weeks, beginning about the middle of July and ending early in August. The course usually covers the techniques of genealogical research, research in various geographical areas and in special fields, with a day set aside each week for visits to special repositories, such as the D.A.R. Library in Memorial Continental Hall in Washington, the Maryland Hall of Records in Annapolis, and the Virginia State Archives in Richmond. Each registrant works on a project, either one of his own problems or some special field in which he has an interest. For detailed instructions about the institute and the forms necessary for registration, you should write to the National Archives and Records Service, General Services Administration, Washington, D.C. 20408. It is advisable to write in the late winter or early spring, rather than wait until June!

There are many other seminars and short courses offered in different parts of the country. The Indiana Historical Society sponsors a day-long seminar in Indianapolis in May or June. The central New York genealogical group usually has one in the spring, sometimes in Syracuse, sometimes in other cities in the area (the Genealogy and Local History Division in the Syracuse Public Library is usually active in planning the meeting, which sometimes lasts two days). Other regional and state groups plan something of the sort. Probably your librarian, state historical society, or state librarian can help you locate such a meeting in your own area.

At least one large university, the Brigham Young University, in Provo, Utah, offers a special course of studies in genealogy and research techniques as part of a four-year course leading to a degree. Write to the Supervisor, Genealogy Technical Research Program, Brigham Young University, Provo, Utah 84601 for detailed information.

The Genealogical Society of the Church of Jesus Christ of Latter-day Saints sponsored and conducted a World Conference on Records in 1969, which about 7000 people attended, and since then, I understand, has held other smaller conferences and seminars. The address is the Genealogical Society, 107 South Main Street, Salt Lake City, Utah 84111. If you think you would like to see one of the finest cities in the United States and use the largest and most comprehensive collection of primary source material in the world, such a seminar would give you an excuse to gratify your wish. Even if there is no seminar, a trip to Salt Lake City to search for ancestors, wherever you think they lived, is well worth while. The hospitality and atmosphere of fellowship there are truly remarkable.

One of the valuable results of such courses is fellowship with other hunters and the opportunity to talk over with them some of your problems. Even clarifying a problem in your own mind in order to state it clearly to someone else helps you to see it more objectively. And sometimes to have a day or week or two in which to do nothing but pursue an elusive ancestor is fun and refreshing.

The Spacing of Generations

Questions are sometimes asked about the number of generations which are likely to occur in a given span of years, say a century. We generally figure three or four generations to a hundred years—in rare instances only two, in others five. The average span between one generation and the next is about twenty-five to thirty years, so, in the space of 350 years, you can estimate that there will be about twelve generations. At the tercentenary of the landing of the Pilgrims at Plymouth most of the applicants for membership in the Society of Mayflower Descendants were of the 10th generation in descent, few were of the 9th, few of the 12th.

There are, of course, exceptions to any rule of thumb. Only a short time ago I read in the newspaper about a boy of twelve who was willing to help support his new-born child whose mother was thirteen. Occasionally one hears of other instances of extraordinarily youthful parentage. Maurice Berkeley, who later became Lord Berkeley, was born in 1281 and married in 1289 at the age of eight to the heiress of considerable property who was also eight. Their first child, Thomas, was born about 1291: he was thirty-five when he succeeded his father in the peerage. His son, another Maurice, also married at the age of eight another heiress, but this young couple was not permitted to live together for several years.

In the days of increasing longevity and youthful marriages, one quite frequently sees in the newspapers pictures of "five generations"—say a great-great-grandmother seated in the center of a group, holding an infant in her arms. She is usually in her eighties, if not her nineties, and the infant is a few months old. Five generations in less than a century! True, but the span between each generation is still twenty to thirty years. Say the great-great grandmother was born in 1880; her son, the great-grandfather, in 1905; his daughter, the grandmother, in 1927; her daughter, the mother, in 1948; and the infant himself in 1970.

At the other extreme, it is not unusual for a man to be forty, fifty, or even sixty before he marries or his first child is born; and in rare, but none the less authentic, cases an octogenarian may father children. The late Richard T. Ely, a noted economist, was born in 1854. He married his second wife in 1931 when he was seventy-seven. Before he died in 1943 he had fathered a son and a daughter by that wife, the youngest born when he was about eighty-four years old—two generations in eighty-four years!

Names

Because I am occasionally asked about surnames, their meaning or origin, I shall take a little space (beyond the mention in Chapter One) to briefly introduce the subject, knowing full well that what I write is but a mere shadow of what you should know if you become really interested in the subject.

Surnames did not come into general use until about the thirteenth and fourteenth centuries, although there are traces of them much before that. The earlier names were usually locative in that they referred to a place on the map. Such names as De Courtenay (later just Courtenay) indicated that the men so called were of the noble family ruling a region and having a chateau of that name in France. Descendants, who came to England in the days of the early Norman kings, kept the designation of their "home town" as their name. This type of name belongs to one of the four main classes of surnames as the specialists in the study of names arrange them. It is called *toponym* and has two subclasses, the locative, derived from the name of a place as Courtenay is, and the topographical, derived from the designation of a physical or geographical feature, such as Hill or Wood. Another class consists of patronymics, rarely metronymics, names inherited from the father like Johnson, Adams (that is, Adam's son, the suffix having been dropped somewhere over the centuries). Another class is the occupational surname, derived from the occupation of the bearer, such as Chandler (candlemaker), Sherman (shear man, one who sheared cloth: note that shearer was one who sheared sheep). The fourth class is made up of nicknames, pet names, diminutives. Many names which seem strange to us today fall in this class, such as Calef (a calf), White or Blount (a blond), Tubbe (a fish found off the coast of Cornwall, where there was a family of this name). There are some names which may be classified in two categories, such as Robinson (Robin, a nickname or diminutive for Robert, to which the patronymic suffix has been added).

Changes in spelling through the years have so altered the original form of some names that it is difficult to discover the earliest form and hence the meaning, unless one is a scholar versed in onomatology (the history of names). Therefore, it is best to consult a good book on the subject. The best, a combination of an excellent and readable essay on surnames and a lengthy list, is the late P. H. Reaney's *A Dictionary of British Surnames* (1961). Dr. Reaney's "dictionary" is not as extensive as we might wish, although it runs to several hundred pages. It does not include many Irish or Scottish names. For the Scottish see George Black's *The Surnames of Scotland,* published as a bulletin of the New York Public Library in 1966; and for the Irish, Edward MacLysaght's *The Surnames of Ireland,* published in Shannon, Ireland, by the Irish University Press, in 1969. The latter is not as comprehensive as Dr. Black's.

There is always a tendency among us amateurs to make assumptions, it being our very nature. However, assumptions in genealogy, especially in claiming relationship because of identity of family names, are treacherous. As Dr. Black observes in his discussion of the name Stewart (Stuart and any other spelling), many noblemen, as well as successive sovereigns, had stewards. Steward (Stewart) is an occupational surname. Stewards were not uncommon in noble households in both England and Scotland. Hence the word may have become a surname almost simultaneously in different areas. Therefore not all Stewarts (Stuarts, etc.) are Scots, nor do they all descend from a common progenitor, or even a family of stewards, although the office of steward was sometimes hereditary. So it is with many other surnames. In my own case (the name means a dune, or hill), I have found Doanes whose name was originally Dohn, the progenitor of whom came from Germany, and others who came from various parts of England and Scotland, some spelling the name Don, some Doun, some Doone, any of which may be transformed into Doan or Doane as some have. So do not rely upon the name alone.

CHAPTER FOURTEEN

Getting Ready to Cross the Atlantic

"How do I go about finding my ancestors in the old country?" This question has been asked quite often by those who have written to me or talked to me about searching for ancestors.

All I can do in helping you with this problem is to suggest what you can do before you initiate any research overseas, and call your attention to one or two sources of more specific direction which will tell you better than I can what to do when you are ready to start searching overseas. In other words, there is a certain amount of hunting which you must do right here in the United States, and there are places to which you can write for records once you have gathered as many facts as you can.

Your very first step, regardless of the nationality of your immigrant progenitor, is to marshal all the facts and traditions which you can collect from your relatives, whether by personal interview or by correspondence. You may find that you should do a little traveling in the United States before you plan to cross the seas; and, if you are able to get to Salt Lake City, you may be able to do a considerable amount of digging right there, where the Genealogical Society has microfilm copies of many overseas records and genealogists who are trained to read them. It also has publications on genealogical research in several countries, including a handbook for many of the English counties or shires, giving location of the archives office and other repositories, if any.

From your own family records, you need to assemble all the facts you can and arrange them in clear and logical order. From your own knowledge, or perhaps from your grandfather or great-aunt you know or learn that your progenitor was an Englishman. Perhaps there is a vague recollection that your grandfather, before he died, said that he came from northern England, but beyond that, when you commence your search, about all you know is that his name was Thomas Ackroyd. That much has been handed down!

Interview as many of the older relatives as you can, and quiz them about any old letters or papers which they may have. If they won't let you take that bundle of old letters home to read at your leisure, go through them then and there and note carefully the names of all persons and places mentioned in each letter, and the date of the letter itself, the name of the writer and of the recipient. One of your older cousins, perhaps, adds a piece to the puzzle when she tells you that her mother said that the family came from Yorkshire; but another cousin tells you that his father said they came from Liverpool. As you poke around you find that many of the nineteenth-century emigrants from England sailed from Liverpool, so both of these cousins may have been right, and Thomas Ackroyd was a Yorkshireman who sailed from that port. Then you pick up the story that he landed in New York on the Fourth of July and was "rather" surprised at the celebration which he found in progress. But as yet you know nothing about his age when he came, or even the year in which he arrived.

But you do know that the family has lived in Wisconsin for four or five generations, so you begin to search for records of them. You find in the State Historical Society the 1850 census and a card index to it which tells you that in the township of Vienna, Dane County, there was, in 1850, a Thomas Ackroyd who was the head of a family, and another Thomas Ackroyd who was younger and single and working as a laborer on a farm. One of your problems now is to distinguish between these two. As a hypothesis you settle on the head of a family and begin to analyze the record. You note that Thomas and his wife Mary and the two eldest children in their family were born in England before 1840, and that the next five children were born in Wisconsin between 1840 and 1850.

The significant fact is that sometime between 1838, when the younger of the two older children was born, and 1840, when the first child born in Wisconsin arrived, the family must have come to the state. As you look at the records of other families in the township, you find that there are several of English origin, and the same pattern prevails in some of them—sometime between 1838 or 1839 and 1840 or 1841 each came to Wisconsin. So it appears that there was a group of English immigrants which probably came together. Note the names (at least the surnames) of these, for they may be useful to you in identifying the ship on which they came and even the community in England from which they came.

Then some fine day you drive out from Milwaukee, where your family has lived for two generations, and see what you can find in Norway Grove, the most central village in the township of Vienna. At least you will visit the cemeteries and perhaps you can find the gravestone of Thomas Ackroyd. At the grocery store in the small village you find a man who tells you that there are still descendants of some of the English families left there and that old Miss Green up the road a half a mile knows more about them than anyone else, because she was related to some of them. You go and talk with her and she gives you an earful indeed! The main facts which you glean from her are that there was a "shipload" of Englishmen and their families who came to Vienna in the summer of 1840, for they had landed in New York on the Fourth of July and come straight out to Wisconsin. She recollects that her grandmother told her that the ship was called the *Aniseed*, which always struck her as odd, naming a ship after a plant seed. She, too, thought that the ship sailed from Liverpool, but her own people were from Yorkshire. You ask her about cemeteries and she tells you where most of the English families were buried, and that you will find some of the Ackroyds there, although most of the family left Vienna before she was born.

In the cemetery you are somewhat disappointed. But you do find the gravestones of Thomas Ackroyd and his wife Mary and two or three other Ackroyds whose names you recognize from the census records, and you carefully copy the inscriptions. You look at the other stones of the same general period, and you find more names which you have seen in the census records. One of them, quite near the Ackroyd stones, is that of John Darcy, who was born in York, England, 16 February 1818 and died 6 August 1885. Some of the others have had the words "born in England" on them, but Thomas Ackroyd's gives merely the date of his death and his age at that time, so you can figure about when he was born, say 1810.

Your next step, now that you have some definite dates, is to search the newspapers of that area—the county weeklies are more likely to carry obituary notices of the inhabitants of the countryside and the small villages and towns than the city dailies are. In one of these you find an obituary notice of Thomas Ackroyd which states that he came to the county in 1840, bringing with him his wife and two children, his nephew Thomas, and his wife's brother, John Darcy. His age checks pretty closely with that given in the 1850 census. So you have him pretty well pinpointed.

You may summarize the facts which you have gathered: You have your ancestor's name and age, his wife's name, the names of the children who were born in England, and you may assume that his wife was a Darcy, since her brother, John Darcy, came with them. You may assume also that the ship on which they came was named something that sounds like *Aniseed,* and that it sailed from Liverpool and arrived in New York about the Fourth of July, 1840.

This last you should verify by writing to the National Archives and Record Service, General Services Administration, Washington, D.C. 20408, and asking if such a ship arrived at that time and if so, was Thomas Ackroyd a passenger. If your date is correct and there was such a ship, an assistant in the National Archives will check the record for you. But suppose that he writes back that they were unable to find such a ship listed, or it didn't arrive that week. You can employ a professional searcher to check the lists of passengers on ships which did arrive about that time and he may find that the ship's name was the *Anglesea*—the old lady probably never knew how its name was spelled and remembered only that it sounded like anise seed. Moreover the *Anglesea* docked on 2 July 1840, having sailed from Liverpool with Captain So-and-So as the master.

Even with as much information as this, and it is more than some have been able to gather, you should continue your search on this side of the water. Look for old family letters, the family Bible—it may be in some cousin's hands in California or Texas! Look at any other old books which may have names written on the flyleaves or letters or clippings tucked between their pages. Sometimes a battered old prayer book will turn up and indicate that even though the groups of English families which settled in Vienna in 1840 were Methodists (or Wesleyans) perhaps the Ackroyds had been originally members of the Church of England as this old prayer book indicates. Say it has the name Roger Ackroyd, 1776, written on one of its leaves. Could he have been the father of Thomas? Or the grandfather? You recall that one of Thomas's sons, as given in the census, was R. Ackroyd. His name could have been Roger, rather than Richard, as you guessed it was. This Roger may be an important clue when you get your English genealogist to work for you.

There is another important source which we have overlooked. Just as you think you have gotten about everything you can find and have wearied all your relatives in pumping them for details, you suddenly think of naturalization. Was Thomas Ackroyd ever naturalized? A news item in the evening paper telling about the swearing in of some new citizens at the county courthouse suggests that you find out where the old records of naturalization are. So you get on the trail. You have four names, Thomas Ackroyd and his nephew Thomas, Roger Ackroyd, relationship unknown, but a possible clue, and John Darcy. Perhaps one of these will produce information which will lead you to a specific spot in England, somewhere in Yorkshire, possibly the city of York. Even if the clerk of the court is discouraging, try to find someone who can tell you where the old records are. One of my friends had to use a little "influence" and asked a lawyer friend of her husband's to prod one of the officials; she then learned that what she wanted was in Chicago. More influence was needed to get at it, but she finally found the record and it gave her some valuable information about date and place of birth, etc.

Once you have pinned a man down to a specific parish in England you can write to the vicar and make arrangements to have the parish register searched for baptisms, marriages, and burials—Crockford's *Clerical Directory* will give you the vicar's name. Remember, by English law, he is entitled to a fee for searching his register, which forms párt of his income.

I find I'm going beyond what I intended to write. Let us then summarize what you should do before you think of writing overseas for information. The principles are the same for all countries. You must have names and dates, even though the latter are only approximate. You must try to associate the name with some particular locality, or it will be like finding a needle in a haystack to attempt to locate him. You should have some idea of when he migrated. If you can find the names of his contemporary relatives, it will aid greatly in the search. Put all your facts into a logical order (see pages 133–35 for an example of how to arrange your data about your immigrant ancestor).

Before you go any farther, I suggest that you get hold of a copy of *Genealogical Research: Methods and Sources* (published in 1960 by the American Society of Genealogists; Vol. II, published in 1971, has chapters on Huguenot and Jewish migrations) and read the chapter in Part 4 which pertains to the country from which your man came. This will give you some idea of how to proceed in hunting for the records you want in that particular country, or how to get in touch with the proper authorities or a genealogist there. Some knowledge of the language of the country is a great asset, but it is not impossible to accomplish a great deal without it. Leslie G. Pine's *The Genealogists' Encyclopedia* (1969) has a list of the archives and repositories of records in most of the European countries and many other parts of the world.

Some European countries have published leaflets which will give you considerable information about research in these particular countries: The British Travel Association, 336 Madison Avenue, New York, N.Y. 10017, has published "Tracing Your Ancestors in Britain." The Royal

Norwegian Ministry of Foreign Affairs, Office of Cultural Relations, Oslo, Norway, has a booklet called "How to Trace Your Ancestors in Norway" (written in English). The Royal Ministry for Foreign Affairs, Press and Information Service, Stockholm, Sweden, has a brochure entitled "Finding Your Forefathers: Some Hints for Americans of Swedish Origin." Recently one for the Netherlands was issued. It is possible that other countries have issued similar booklets. There may be a small charge for some of these. You might try writing to the embassy of the country in which you are interested and asking for information—they all have offices in Washington, D.C., which will at least refer your request to the proper official.

L'ENVOI

A Book or Two for Reading and Reference

MANY PEOPLE like to read about their hobby and look for books which feed their enthusiasm and advance their knowledge. So I share with you a few books which have given me both pleasure and profit, and a couple which I have found useful for ready reference.

One of the ablest genealogists of my time was the late Donald Lines Jacobus, 1887–1970, of New Haven, Conn., generally called the "Dean of American Genealogists." He was selected as one of the charter Fellows of the American Society of Genealogists when it was founded in 1940–41. During his long and active life (he began publishing in 1905; his last contribution was published a few months before his death), Mr. Jacobus did more than any other genealogist in the United States to set and exemplify standards for his profession. He was a prolific writer and left a corpus of remarkably authoritative and lasting genealogy. He established and edited the *American Genealogist* (*TAG*), considered one of the ranking journals in the field, and contributed to many other genealogical periodicals. In 1930 he published a collection of his essays, articles, and editorials under the title *Genealogy as Pastime and Profession,* which is now considered a classic in the field. In 1968 a second edition, containing an additional essay, was published by the Genealogical Publishing Co., Baltimore. A memoir of Mr. Jacobus by John Insley Coddington, F.A.S.G., his friend and disciple, was published in the *New England Historical and Genealogical Register,* January 1971. As good and worth-while reading, I commend *Genealogy as Pastime and Profession* to you.

165

Another one of my favorite books is Sir Anthony Wagner's *English Genealogy*, first published in 1960, second enlarged edition, published by the Clarendon Press, Oxford, England, in 1972. Sir Anthony is Garter King-of-Arms and head of the College of Heralds in London. He has written an absorbing account of English genealogy from the coming of the Anglo-Saxons and Vikings to the emigrations to the colonies and United States in the nineteenth century. Many descents, with excellent bibliographical footnotes, are given as examples of the emergence of notable families, their flux and change, rise and fall. He comments on the work of many well-known English genealogists, such as Sir William Dugdale, 1605–86, whose *Baronage* (1675–76) is a monument, and J. Horace Round, 1854–1928, whose pithy and often vitriolic articles did much to lift genealogy out of the slough of "patchwork" and "wishful thinking" and to give it the rank of historical science. A few Americans, among them Colonel Joseph Lemuel Chester, 1821–82, the only American genealogist buried in Westminister Abbey, and the late George Andrews Moriarty, F.A.S.G., 1883–1968, an authority on English medieval genealogy, are also noticed. If you are interested in learning more about your hobby and take genealogy seriously, this book is worth your while. Do not confuse it with his *English Ancestry,* a small how-to-do-it.

I have mentioned above J. Horace Round, who did so much to win respect for genealogy as a profession. There are about half-a-dozen books to his credit, as well as many contributions to dictionaries and encyclopedias, journals, etc. The posthumously published collection of some of his better known essays was published as *Family Origins and Other Studies* (1930, reprinted in Baltimore, 1970). The essay on "Historic Genealogy" in that volume is particularly worth while for the serious genealogist.

Noel C. Stevenson, F.A.S.G., a lawyer in Los Angeles, brought together an anthology of essays by various authors and from various journals, entitled *The Genealogical Reader,* published by the Deseret Book Co., Salt Lake City, in 1958. There are many excellent essays in this volume, among them one or two by Mr. Jacobus which

he omitted from his own book. So here is another book
for your reading shelf.

For quick and ready reference I have found two handbooks of considerable use. One, by Mr. Stevenson, just
mentioned, is entitled *Search and Research* (Salt Lake
City, 1959). I turn to it for the "genealogy" of counties
in the several states. It is sometimes quite important to
your research to know just when each county was organized and set apart from its parent. You may find the
records you are seeking in the courthouse of the parent
county, even though your ancestor always lived on the
same land. The other is *The Handybook for Genealogists*,
published by the Everton Press, Logan, Utah, which has
been revised several times. The copy I use is in the fourth
edition, 1964. There is in it a lot of information of practical use to you in your search.

I call your attention to *Genealogical Research: Methods and Sources* (2 vols., 1960, 1971) published by the
American Society of Genealogists, Washington, D.C.
These two volumes consist of articles written and contributed by Fellows of the society. They deal with methods and sources of record information in several European countries (Vol. I) and a dozen of the midwestern
states in the United States (Vol. II). Membership in this
society is limited to fifty. When the society was founded
in 1940–41, twenty-five genealogists were invited to become Charter Fellows, who then elected more to join
them. Membership is by invitation only. Hence, this is
truly an honorary society.

As I have been revising this book for the fourth edition, I have been debating about leaving out Appendix A,
because P. William Filby, librarian of the Maryland Historical Society in Baltimore, has compiled a much more
extensive bibliography, *American & British Genealogy
& Heraldry* (Chicago, 1970). He covers all fifty states in
the United States, whereas I include only fifteen, those
on the Atlantic Seaboard; therefore his book will be much
more useful to many of my readers who must start their
searching in one or more of the other thirty-five. Also,
Mr. Filby's book has the advantage of being up-to-date,
including many publications which I have never seen,

and providing sections on Canada, England, Ireland, Scotland, and Wales, and on heraldry. However, as I spot-checked the two books where they overlap, I found that I have included some old, useful books, among them several indexes to "buried" genealogy, which, although out-of-date, frequently help in locating data on families about which little has been printed. Therefore, I have decided to reprint Appendix A, with a few additions and revisions here and there.

APPENDIXES AND INDEX

Bibliographies

The following lists of books are not to be regarded as complete and exhaustive bibliographies, but they are intended to serve as a guide to the most used books in each indicated field. The individual starting out to dig for ancestors must remember that no one book can tell him how to work out his lines, for each line presents its own problems. Therefore these lists suggest the starting points for further research in books, once the hunter has reached the point where he can begin to work in printed material. You will note that no histories of individual families are suggested. For references to printed genealogies of specific families you should consult especially the bibliographies listed in sections B and C. Section D lists the better known general magazines of genealogical interest. Section E contains selected bibliographies of the most used books of general interest and for the genealogy of the specified regions. In parentheses following some of the titles are the popular names by which genealogists frequently refer to them.

A. Handbooks and Guides

When *Searching for Your Ancestors* was first published there was scarcely a handbook of genealogical research in print or available even in the secondhand book stores. Now there are many. Those listed below seem to me to be particularly useful for one reason or another.

American Society of Genealogists. *Genealogical Research: Methods and Sources.* 2 vols. Washington, 1960, 1971. (A collection of essays by Fellows of the society. Vol. I: Part 1, General considerations; Part 2, Materials for research; Part 3, Regional genealogy; Part 4, Pre-American ancestry; Part 5, Special fields of investigations. Vol. II: Part 1, Regional genealogy, with essays on eleven midwestern states; Part 2, Special studies—Ontario, Huguenot migrations, Jewish migrations.)

Bennett, Archibald F. *A Guide for Genealogical Research.* Salt Lake City, 1951. (Don't overlook the bibliographies in Appen-

dix II, especially those which pertain to research in foreign
countries, and the foreign genealogical terms in Appendix III.)
————. *Finding Your Forefathers in America.* Salt Lake City,
1957. (In this book, the late Mr. Bennett develops his case history method of instruction and follows a case through, step by
step, to illustrate his points. It is a book for one who has had
some preliminary experience, or at least read his *Guide.*)
————. *Advanced Genealogical Research.* Salt Lake City, 1959.
(Mr. Bennett continues to use the case history method. All
three of these volumes are fully indexed.)
Everton, George B., and Others. *The Handybook for Genealogists.*
Logan, Utah, 1971. 6th ed. (Get the latest available edition.
This is a guide to county and state histories, maps, libraries, etc.
It contains bibliographies and includes Canada and several Eu-
ropean countries.)
Kirkham, E. Kay. *Research in American Genealogy: A Practical
Approach to Genealogical Research.* Salt Lake City, 1956. (An
expansion of the author's *The ABC's of American Genealogical
Research*, 1954. It gives the location of the seats of all the coun-
ties in the United States, and of the provinces of Canada.)
National Genealogical Society. Special publications, as follows:
No. 14, *General Aids to Genealogical Research;* No. 15, *Special
Aids to Genealogical Research on Southern Families;* No. 16,
*Special Aids to Genealogical Research in Northeastern and Cen-
tral States.* (Of the several special publications of this society
these are of particular interest to the general hunter; the others
for the most part deal with special fields or special localities. A
list can be obtained from the society, 1921 Sunderland Place,
N.W., Washington, D.C. 20036.)
Parker, Donald Dean. *Local History, How to Gather It, Write It,
and Publish It.* Revised and edited by Bertha A. Josephson.
New York, 1944. (Useful and suggestive to the experienced
genealogist who wants to follow through and give his history
of a family its full setting.)
Peterson, Clarence Stewart. *The American Pioneer in Forty-Eight
States.* New York, 1945. (Useful for its brief account of the set-
tlement of each of the states then in the Union.)
————. *Bibliography of County Histories in Fifty States in 1961.*
Baltimore, Md., 1963.
Stevenson, Noel C. *The Genealogical Reader: A Collection of Ar-
ticles Selected and Edited.* Salt Lake City, 1958. (Excellent articles on various phases of genealogical research culled from the
leading genealogical journals.)
————. *Search and Research, the Researcher's Handbook: A Guide
to Official Records and Library Sources.* Revised edition. Salt
Lake City, 1959. (There is a great deal of concise information
in the introductory sections which will repay careful reading.
The main part of the book is devoted to locating books and

records in the several states under each of which there is the
same topical arrangement, namely: General Information Li-
braries; Historical Societies and Archives; Research Suggestions;
Reference Books; Military Rosters, Rolls, and Records; Official
Records, including court and probate records; Federal Census
Records; State Census Records.)

United States National Archives. *Guide to Genealogical Records
in the National Archives.* Washington, 1964 (National Archives
Publication No. 49–13. A description of the contents of each
records unit, of limited use to the beginner, but valuable to the
advanced genealogist.)

Williams, Ethel W. *Know Your Ancestors.* Rutland, Vt., 1964. (An
excellent comprehensive guide to genealogical research, with
bibliographies.)

B. Indexes to "Buried" Genealogies

The American Genealogical Index. Edited by Fremont J. Rider.
48 vols. Middletown, Conn., 1942–52. (Indexes the individual
names in a selected list of several hundred family histories and
the federal census of 1790.)

The American Genealogical Biographical Index. Edited by Fremont J. Rider. Middletown, Conn., 1952–. (Continuation of preceding; in process of publication. In addition to more families'
histories, it includes all the names in the *Boston Evening Transcript,* 1906–41, and 63 volumes of lists of Revolutionary War
soldiers and a few other military rosters. I judge that this useful
tool will extend to at least 150 volumes.)

The "Durrie" Series:

*Bibliographia genealogica americana: An Alphabetical Index to
American Genealogies and Pedigrees Contained in State,
County, and Town Histories, Printed Genealogies, and Kindred Works.* By Daniel S. Durrie. Albany, 1868. 2d ed., revised and enlarged. Albany, 1878. 3d ed., revised and enlarged. Albany, 1886 (Supplement, 1888).

*Index to American Genealogies and to Genealogical Material
Contained in All Works Such as Town Histories, County Histories, Local Histories, Historical Society Publications, Biogra-
phies, Historical Periodicals, and Kindred Works.* 4th ed.,
revised, improved, and enlarged, containing nearly 40,000
references. Albany, 1895. 5th ed., revised, improved, and enlarged. Albany, 1900 (Supplement, 1900–8, Albany, 1908).
(*Munsell's Genealogical Index.*)

Munsell's Genealogical Index. South Norwalk, Conn., 1933–.*
(Really the sixth edition.)

The Grafton Index of Books and Magazine Articles on History,

---

* A date expressed in this form indicates that the book series or
periodical is still in process of publication.

Genealogy, and Biography Printed in the United States on American Subjects during the Year 1909. New York, *ca.* 1910.

Jacobus, Donald Lines. *Index to Genealogical Periodicals.* 3 vols. New Haven, 1932–53. (The third volume contains the late Mr. Jacobus's "Own Index," a key to many excellent studies of ancestral lines buried in the lineages of individuals, such as Ferris's *The Dawes-Gates Ancestral Lines.*)

Newberry Library, Chicago. *The Genealogical Index.* 4 vols. Boston, 1960. (Very important for buried accounts.)

C. Bibliographies of Individual Family Histories

Daughters of the American Revolution, Library. Washington, D.C. *Catalogue of Genealogical and Historical Works, Library of the National Society, Daughters of the American Revolution.* Washington, 1940.

Daughters of the American Revolution, Georgia. *Catalogue of the Georgia Society, D.A.R. Library . . . in the Georgia Department of Archives and History.* [Atlanta, 1956.]

Goodspeed's Book Shop, Boston. *Genealogy and Local History.* Boston, 1971. (*Goodspeed List.* This is the latest Goodspeed catalogue to be issued. Previous ones are valuable.)

Long Island Historical Society, Brooklyn, N.Y. *Catalogue of American Genealogies.* Brooklyn, 1935. (*The Long Island List.* It contains a list of over 8000 genealogies.)

Public Library, St. Louis, Mo. *Catalogue of Genealogical Material and Local Histories.* Revised edition. St. Louis, 1953.

United States Library of Congress, Washington, D.C. *American and English Genealogies in the Library of Congress.* 2d ed. Washington, 1919. (*The L.C. List.* Note: in 1971 the card catalogue of the genealogies in the Library of Congress was copied on microfilm to serve as a "third" edition of this. It is available in subscribing libraries.)

D. Current Magazines and Serials of General Interest

American Genealogist (formerly *New Haven Genealogical Magazine*). New Haven (now Des Moines, Iowa), 1923–. (*TAG.*)

National Genealogical Society Quarterly. 1912–. (*N.G.S.*)

New England Historical and Genealogical Register. 1847–. (The *Register.*)

New York Genealogical and Biographical Record. 1870–. (The *Record.*)

E. Some Important Sources of Genealogical Data

It should be emphasized that this is a list of selected titles, and that it makes no pretension of being complete. A complete bibliography of the genealogical source material in print would call for a good-sized volume for each state and is, therefore, out of place in this book. Only material for the thirteen original states and Vermont and Maine has been selected. New England is so integral a section of the country that the more general works pertaining to it as a whole have been given a separate classification.

Many ancestor hunters are but a few generations removed from the Atlantic Seaboard, sometimes but one or two, so this list is designed as a "first aid" to them when once they begin to work in genealogical libraries. Experts will undoubtedly miss some of their favorite reference books, but they should remember that this list is intended to introduce newcomers to the books with which they should become acquainted: except incidentally, it is not a bibliography for the advanced or professional genealogist.

Little effort has been made to revise this section for the fourth edition of this volume because P. William Filby's *American & British Genealogy & Heraldry* (Chicago, 1970) is a comprehensive bibliography containing references for all the fifty states as well as the British Isles. It should be used, when available in your local library, in preference to the following.

Again the popular names for some of these books are indicated in parentheses placed after the official titiles.

1. GENERAL

American-Irish Historical Society. *Journal*. New York, 1898–.

Baird, Charles Washington. *History of the Huguenot Emigration to America.* 2 vols. New York, 1885. (*Baird's Huguenots*.)

Bardsley, Charles Wareing Endell. *Curiosities of Puritan Nomenclature.* New York, London, 1880. (Later edition, 1897.)

———. *A Dictionary of English and Welsh Surnames, with Special American Instances.* London and New York, 1901. (A revised edition of his *English Surnames*.)

Blegen, Theodore Christian. *Norwegian Migration to America.* Northfield, Minn., 1931.

Bolton, Charles Knowles. *Scotch Irish Pioneers in Ulster and America.* Boston, 1910.

Browning, Charles Henry. *Americans of Royal Descent.* 7th ed. Philadelphia, 1911. (The pedigrees contained in this volume must be carefully checked with source material.)

Burke, Sir John Bernard. *Burke's Genealogical and Heraldic History of the Landed Gentry, including American Families with British Ancestry.* London, 1939. (*Burke's Landed Gentry.* Must be used with care. The American supplement, an innovation in this edition, contains several hundred pedigrees, but the English connection should not be accepted without checking against documentary authorities. For English landed families now extinct consult earlier editions.)

———. *A Genealogical and Heraldic History of the Peerage and Baronetage, the Privy Council, and Knightage.* 93d ed. London, 1935. (*Burke's Peerage.* Should be used with care. Contains only peerages now in existence.)

―――. *The General Armory of England, Scotland, Ireland, and Wales; Comprising a Registry of Armorial Bearings from the Earliest to the Present Time.* London, 1884, reprinted 1969. (*Burke's Armory.* One of many lists and descriptions of coats of arms.)

The Complete Peerage. Edited by Vicary Gibbs. 13 vols. in 14. London, 1910–59. (The most authoritative peerage. Contains extinct and dormant as well as extant peerages.)

Crozier, William Armstrong. *A Registry of American Families Entitled to Coat Armor.* New York, 1904.

Emigrants from England, 1773–76. Boston, 1913. (Reprinted from the *Register,* Vols. 62–65.)

Faust, Albert Bernhardt. *The German Element in the United States.* New York, 1927.

―――. *Lists of Swiss Emigrants in the Eighteenth Century to the American Colonies.* 2 vols. Washington, 1920–25.

Ford, Henry Jones. *The Scotch-Irish in America.* Princeton, 1915.

Fosdick, Lucian John. *The French Blood in America.* New York, 1911.

Gates, Susa (Young). *Surname Book and Racial History: A Compilation and Arrangement of Genealogical and Historical Data for Use by the Students and Members of the Relief Society of the Church of Jesus Christ of Latter-day Saints.* Salt Lake City, 1918.

The Handbook of American Genealogy. 4 vols. Chicago, 1932–43. (Includes bibliographies and *Who's Who in Genealogy.* A very useful reference guide.)

Harrison, Henry. *Surnames of the United Kingdom.* 2 vols. London, 1912–18.

Hotten, John Camden. *The Original Lists of Persons of Quality . . . Who Went from Great Britain to the American Plantations, 1600–1700.* New York, 1880. (*Hotten's List.*)

Lancour, Adlore Harold. *Passenger List of Ships Coming to North America, 1607–1825.* New York, 1937. (Also published in *New York Public Library Bulletin.* Vol. 41, May 1937, pp. 389–410. A very useful bibliography.)

List of Emigrants to America from Liverpool, 1697–1707. Boston, 1913. (Reprinted from the *Register,* Vols. 64–65.)

McGee, Thomas D'Arcy. *A History of the Irish Settlers in North America, from the Earliest Period to the Census of 1850.* 5th ed. Boston, 1852.

MacLean, John Patterson. *An Historical Account of the Settlements of Scotch Highlanders in America prior to the Peace of 1783.* Cleveland and Glasgow, 1900.

Marvin, George Ritchie. *The Genealogical Directory, 1931.* Boston, 1931. (A list of genealogists and genealogical associations now out of date and in need of thorough revision.)

Virkus, Frederick Adams. *The Abridged Compendium of American*

Genealogy. 7 vols. Chicago, 1925–42. (The Compendium. Should be used with care.)

Waters, Henry Fitz Gilbert. *Genealogical Gleanings in England.* 2 vols. Boston, 1901. (Supplemented by articles in the *Register,* largely by the Committee on English and Foreign Research.)

2. NEW ENGLAND

Bodge, George Madison. *Soldiers in King Philip's War.* 3d ed. Boston, 1906.

Bolton, Mrs. Ethel (Stanwood). *Immigrants to New England, 1700–75.* Salem, 1931.

Cutter, William Richard. *New England Families, Genealogical and Memorial.* 4 vols. New York, 1913. (This and the next two titles should be used with care and checked against other authorities.)

————. *New England Families, Genealogical and Memorial.* 4 vols. New York, 1914.

————. *New England Families, Genealogical and Memorial.* 3d series. New York, 1915.

Drake, Samuel Gardner. *Result of Some Researches among the British Archives for Information Relative to the Founders of New England.* Boston, 1860.

Holmes, Frank R. *Directory of the Ancestral Heads of New England Families, 1620–1700.* New York, 1923.

Mather, Cotton. *Magnalia Christi Americana; or, The Ecclesiastical History of New England.* 2 vols. Hartford, 1853–55. (*Mather's Magnalia.* Important source material. This is the best edition for the genealogist since it contains an index.)

Pierce, Ebenezer Weaver. *Pierce's Colonial Lists: Civil, Military and Professional Lists of Plymouth and Rhode Island Colonies, 1621–1700.* Boston, 1881.

Savage, James. *A Genealogical Dictionary of the First Settlers of New England, Showing Three Generations of Those Who Came before May, 1692.* 4 vols. Boston, 1860–62. (With this should be used O. P. Dexter's *A Genealogical Cross Index of . . . Savage* and Mrs. C. W. Dall's *Genealogical Notes and Errata to Savage's Genealogical Dictionary.* Known as *Savage.* Very valuable, but needs revision. Should be checked against later authorities.)

3. CONNECTICUT

Bailey, Frederic William. *Early Connecticut Marriages as Found on Ancient Church Records prior to 1800.* 7 vols. New Haven, 1896–1906. (By no means complete, but very useful.)

Barbour Collection of Connecticut Vital Records. (The index, on cards, to this great collection has been copied on microfilm and may be found in the following libraries: Genealogical Society of Utah, Salt Lake City; State Historical Society of Wisconsin, Madison; Burton Historical Collection, Detroit Public Library;

and the Daughters of the American Revolution Library, Washington, D.C. The original collection is in the Connecticut State Library, where many other Connecticut records have been collected.)

Connecticut (Colony). *The Public Records of the Colony of Connecticut, 1636–1776.* 15 vols. Hartford, 1850–90.

Connecticut. *The Public Records of the State of Connecticut.* 3 vols. Hartford, 1894–1922.

Connecticut Historical Society, Hartford. *Collections.* Hartford, 1860–. (Useful documents.)

Connecticut Magazine. 12 vols. Hartford, 1895–1908.

Cutter, William Richard. *Genealogical and Family History of the State of Connecticut.* 4 vols. New York, 1911. (Should be used with care and checked against other authorities.)

Encyclopedia of Connecticut Biography, Genealogical-Memorial. 4 vols. Boston and New York, 1917. (Should be used with care and checked against other authorities.)

Flagg, Charles Allcott. *Reference List on Connecticut Local History.* Albany, 1900. (An old but still useful bibliography.)

Goodwin, Nathaniel. *Genealogical Notes, or Contributions to the Family History of Some of the First Settlers of Connecticut and Massachusetts.* Hartford, 1856.

Hinman, Royal Ralph. *A Catalogue of the Names of the Early Puritan Settlers of the Colony of Connecticut.* Hartford, 1852–56. (*Hinman's Catalogue.* Goes only through "Dani.")

Jacobus, Donald Lines. *List of Officials, Civil, Military, and Ecclesiastical of Connecticut Colony, from March 1636 through 11 October 1677, and of New Haven Colony throughout Its Separate Existence; Also Soldiers in the Pequot War Who Then or Subsequently Resided within the Present Bounds of Connecticut.* New Haven, 1935.

Manwaring, Charles William. *A Digest of the Early Connecticut Probate Records.* 3 vols. Hartford, 1904–6.

Mather, Frederick Gregory. *The Refugees of 1776 from Long Island to Connecticut.* Albany, 1913.

New Haven Colony Historical Society. *Papers.* New Haven, 1865–.

Shepard, James. *Connecticut Soldiers in the Pequot War of 1637.* Meriden, Conn., 1913.

United States Bureau of the Census. *Heads of Families at the First Census of the United States Taken in the Year 1790: Connecticut.* Washington, 1908.

4. DELAWARE

Delaware Historical Society. *Papers of the Historical Society of Delaware.* 1879–.

Delaware Public Archives Commission. *Delaware Archives.* 1911–.

Louhi, Evert Alexander. *The Delaware Finns.* New York, 1925.

National Society of the Colonial Dames of America, Delaware. *A Calendar of Delaware Wills, New Castle County.* 1911.

Scharf, John Thomas. *History of Delaware, 1609–1888.* 2 vols. 1888.

Turner, Charles Henry Black. *Rodney's Diary and Other Delaware Records.* 1911.

5. GEORGIA

The Colonial Records of the State of Georgia. 1904–.

Daughters of the American Revolution, Georgia. *Historical Collections of the Georgia Chapters.* Atlanta, 1926–. (An index to Vol. 1 was published in 1931.)

――――. *Historical Collections of the Joseph Habersham Chapter.* 3 vols. 1902–10.

Davis, Harry Alexander. *Some Huguenot Families of South Carolina and Georgia.* 1927.

Gilmer, George Rockingham. *Sketches of Some of the First Settlers of Upper Georgia.* 1855.

National Society of the Colonial Dames of America, Georgia. *Some Early Epitaphs in Georgia.* 1924.

Strobel, Philip A. *The Salzburgers and Their Descendants.* 1855.

6. MAINE

Libby, Charles Thornton. *Genealogical Dictionary of Maine and New Hampshire.* 1928–39. (A very valuable work.)

Little, George Thomas. *Genealogical and Family History of the State of Maine.* 4 vols. 1909. (Must be used with care and checked against original records.)

Maine Genealogist and Biographer, A Quarterly Journal. 3 vols. 1875–78.

Maine Historical and Genealogical Recorder. 9 vols. 1884–98.

Maine Historical Society. *Collections.* 1st, 2d, and 3d series. 1831–.

――――. *Documentary History of the State of Maine.* 24 vols. 1869–1916.

Pope, Charles Henry. *The Pioneers of Maine and New Hampshire, 1623 to 1660.* 1908.

Sargent, William Mitchell. *Maine Wills, 1640–1760.* 1887.

Spencer, Wilbur Daniel. *Pioneers on Maine Rivers, with Lists to 1651.* 1930.

Sprague's Journal of Maine History. 14 vols. 1913–26.

United States Bureau of the Census. *Heads of Families at the First Census, 1790: Maine.* 1908.

7. MARYLAND

Bromwell, Henrietta Elizabeth. *Old Maryland Families: A Collection of Charts Compiled from Public Records, Wills, Family Bibles, Tomb Inscriptions, and Other Original Sources.* 1916.

Brumbaugh, Gaius Marcus. *Maryland Records, Colonial, Revolutionary, County and Church, from Original Sources.* 1915.
————. *Revolutionary Records of Maryland.* 1924.
Cotton, Mrs. Jane (Baldwin). *The Maryland Calendar of Wills.* 8 vols. 1901–28.
Magruder, James Mosby. *Index of Maryland Colonial Wills, 1634–1777 at Land Office, Annapolis, Md.* 3 vols. *ca.* 1933.
————. *Magruder's Maryland Colonial Abstracts: Wills, Accounts and Inventories. ca.* 1934.
Maryland Genealogical Bulletin. January 1930–.
Maryland Historical Magazine. March 1906–.
Neill, Edward Duffield. *The Founders of Maryland as Portrayed in Manuscripts, Provincial Records and Early Documents.* 1876.
Passano, Eleanor Phillips. *An Index to the Source Records of Maryland: Genealogical, Biographical and Historical.* Baltimore, 1940.
Richardson, Mrs. Hester (Dorsey). *Side-lights on Maryland History, with Sketches of Early Maryland Families.* 2 vols. 1913.
Ridgely, Helen West. *A Calendar of Memorial Inscriptions Collected in the State of Maryland.* 1906.
————. *Historic Graves of Maryland and the District of Columbia.* 1908.
Scharf, John Thomas. *History of Maryland from the Earliest Period to the Present Day.* 3 vols. 1879.
————. *History of Western Maryland.* 2 vols. 1882.
Skirven, Percy Granger. *The First Parishes of the Province of Maryland. ca.* 1923.
United States Bureau of the Census. *Heads of Families at the First Census of the United States Taken in the Year 1790: Maryland.* 1907.

8. MASSACHUSETTS

Andrews, Henry Franklin. *List of Freemen, Massachusetts Bay Colony from 1630 to 1691.* 1906.
Bailey, Frederick William. *Early Massachusetts Marriages prior to 1800.* 3 vols. 1897–.
Banks, Charles Edward. *The English Ancestry and Homes of the Pilgrim Fathers. ca.* 1929.
————. *The Planters of the Commonwealth: A Study of the Emigrants and Emigration in Colonial Times.* 1930.
————. *Topographical Dictionary of 2885 English Emigrants to New England, 1620–50.* 1937. (Largely Massachusetts families.)
————. *The Winthrop Fleet of 1630.* 1930.
Bowditch, Nathaniel Ingersoll. *Suffolk Surnames.* 3d ed. 1861.
Bowen, Richard LeBaron. *Massachusetts Records: A Handbook for Genealogists, Historians [etc.].* Rehoboth, Mass., 1957. (A guide to the towns and counties, with an indication of those whose records have been published.)

Bowman, George Ernest. *The Mayflower Compact and Its Signers.* Boston, 1920. (The authoritative list by the outstanding authority.)

Colonial Society of Massachusetts. *Publications.* 1892– (An index to Vols. 1–25 was published in 1932.)

Crane, Ellery Bicknell. *Historic Homes and Institutions and Genealogical and Personal Memoirs of Worcester County, Massachusetts.* 4 vols. 1907. (Should be used with care, but useful because of early generations of Massachusetts families.)

Cutter, William Richard. *Genealogical and Personal Memoirs Relating to the Families of Boston and Eastern Massachusetts.* 4 vols. 1908. (Should be used with care.)

————. *Genealogical and Personal Memoirs Relating to the Families of the State of Massachusetts.* 4 vols. 1910. (Should be used with care.)

————. *Historic Homes and Places and Genealogical and Personal Memoirs Relating to the Families of Middlesex County Massachusetts.* 4 vols. 1908. (Should be used with care, but useful for early Massachusetts families.)

Dedham Historical Register. 14 vols. 1890–1903.

Essex Antiquarian. 13 vols. 1897–1909. (See also the *Massachusetts Magazine.*)

Essex Institute. *Historical Collections.* 1859–. (Very valuable for Essex County.)

Flagg, Charles Allcott. *A Guide to Massachusetts Local History.* 1907. (Still useful, but many local histories have been published since 1907.)

————. *An Index of Pioneers from Massachusetts to the West.* 1915.

The Historical and Genealogical Researches and Recorder of Passing Events of Merrimack Valley. 1 vol. 1857–58.

Hurd, Charles Edwin. *Genealogy and History of Representative Citizens of the Commonwealth of Massachusetts.* 1902.

Massachusetts (Colony and Province). *Records of the Governor and Company of Massachusetts Bay in New England.* 5 vols. in 6. 1853–54.

Massachusetts Historical Society. *Collections.* 1792–.

————. *Proceedings.* 1859–.

Massachusetts Magazine. 11 vols. in 10. 1908–18.

Mayflower Descendant. 34 vols. 1899–1937. (Very valuable for the Cape Cod area. A consolidated index appeared in 1959, edited by G. E. Bowman—see above.)

Pope, Charles Henry. *The Pioneers of Massachusetts.* 1900 (*Pope's Pioneers.*)

————. *The Plymouth Scrap-book.* 1918.

Sewall, Samuel. *The Diary of Samuel Sewall.* 1674–1729. (In Massachusetts Historical Society, *Collections,* series 5, Vols. 5–7, 1878–82.)

Shaw, Hubert Kinsey. *Families of the Pilgrims*. Boston, 1956. (A
carefully compiled record of all known descendants of the
passengers on the *Mayflower* through the third generation, sponsored by the Massachusetts Society of Mayflower Descendants.
This will be superseded by the "Five-Generation Project" of the
General Society of Mayflower Descendants, when that is completed.)

Suffolk County, Mass. *Suffolk Deeds.* 14 vols. 1880–1906.

United States Bureau of the Census. *Heads of Families at the
First Census of the United States Taken in the Year 1790:
Massachusetts.* 1908.

Whitmore, William Henry. *The Massachusetts Civil List for the
Colonial and Provincial Periods, 1630–1774.* 1870.

Willison, George Findlay. *The Pilgrim Reader: The story of the
Pilgrims as Told by Themselves & Their Contemporaries,
Friendly & Unfriendly.* New York, 1953. (A selection of origi
nal documents, with an appendix, "The Pilgrim Company," re
printed from the following title.)

————. *Saints and Strangers: Being the Lives of the Pilgrim
Fathers & Their Families, with Their Friends & Foes, on Ac-
count of Their Posthumous Wanderings in Limbo, Their Final
Resurrection & Rise to Glory, & the Strange Pilgrimages of
Plymouth Rock.* New York, 1945. (The most readable account
of the early days of the Plymouth Colony; the appendix, "The
Pilgrim Company," gives the names of all who have been iden-
tified as coming on the first seven ships, including the second
Mayflower, 1620–30. Read with this the "novel" by Ernest
Gebler, *The Plymouth Adventure,* Garden City, N.Y., 1950,
which is the story of the voyage of the *Mayflower,* 1620.)

9. NEW HAMPSHIRE

Granite Monthly. April 1877–.

National Society of the Colonial Dames of America, N.H. *Gravestone Inscriptions Gathered . . . in the State of New Hampshire.*
1913.

New Hampshire (Colony). *Probate Records of the Province of
New Hampshire.* 1907–41. (Covers 1635 to 1771, when the
province was divided into counties.)

New Hampshire. *Provincial and State Papers.* 1867–.

New Hampshire Antiquarian Society. *Collections.* 4 numbers in
1 vol. 1874–79.

New Hampshire Genealogical Record. 7 vols. 1903–10.

New Hampshire Historical Society. *Collections.* 1824–.

————. *Proceedings.* 1874–.

New Hampshire Repository. 2 vols. 1846–47.

Stearns, Ezra Scollay. *Genealogical and Family History of the
State of New Hampshire.* 4 vols. 1908. (Use with care.)

United States Bureau of the Census. *Heads of Families at the*

First Census of the United States Taken in the Year 1790: New Hampshire. 1907.

10. NEW JERSEY

Chambers, Theodore Frelinghuysen. *The Early Germans of New Jersey: Their History, Churches and Genealogies.* 1895.

Documents Relating to the Colonial History of the State of New Jersey. 1880–. (New Jersey Archives.)

Documents Relating to the Revolutionary History of the State of New Jersey. 5 vols. 1901–17. (The second series of the New Jersey Archives.)

Genealogical Magazine of New Jersey. 1925–.

Lee, Francis Bazley. *Genealogical and Memorial History of the State of New Jersey.* 4 vols. 1910. (Must be used with care, and checked against original records.)

———. *New Jersey as a Colony and as a State.* 4 vols. 1902.

Littell, John. *Family Records; or Genealogies of the First Settlers of Passaic Valley.* 1851.

Nelson, William. *Calendar of New Jersey Wills.* 1901. (In *Documents Relating to the Colonial History of the State of New Jersey*, Vol. 23.)

———. *Church Records in New Jersey.* 1904. (A bibliography of church records.)

———. *Marriage Records, 1665–1800.* 1900. (In *Documents Relating to the Colonial History of the State of New Jersey*, Vol. 22.)

New Jersey, Division of the State Library, Archives, and History. *Genealogical Research: A Guide to Source Materials in the New Jersey State Library and Other State Agencies.* Trenton, 1957. (A useful guide which includes suggestions of other sources.)

New Jersey Historical Society. *Proceedings.* 1845–. (An index to the first 36 volumes has been published.)

Somerset County Historical Quarterly. 8 vols. 1912–19.

Stillwell, John Edwin. *Historical and Genealogical Miscellany: Data Relating to the Settlement and Settlers of New York and New Jersey.* 4 vols. 1903–15.

11. NEW YORK

Gunther E. Pohl, Genealogy and Local History Reference Room, New York Public Library, Fifth Avenue and 42nd Street, New York, N.Y. 10018, has compiled an index of some 800 volumes of New York local and county histories, biographical "albums," etc., amounting to about a quarter of a million names. For a small fee he is willing to give you up to ten references to a specific name. In some of those albums and histories a certain amount of genealogy is given, so this may be a helpful source.

Albany County, N.Y. *Early Records of the City and County of*

Albany, and Colony of Rensselaerwyck. 1869–. (Deeds, notarial records, mortgages, and wills.)

Anjou, Gustave. *Ulster County, N.Y., Probate Records.* 1906–.

Bailey, Rosalie Fellows. *Guide to Genealogical and Biographical Sources for New York City (Manhattan), 1783–1898.* New York, 1954. (Valuable for those who want to know where to find records in a complex municipal government organization.)

Bergen, Teunis G. *Register in Alphabetical Order, of the Early Settlers of Kings County, Long Island.* 1881.

Cutter, William Richard. *Genealogical and Family History of Central New York.* 3 vols. 1912. (Must be used with care and checked against original records.)

——. *Genealogical and Family History of Northern New York.* 3 vols. 1910. (Must be used with care and checked against original records.)

——. *Genealogical and Family History of Southern New York.* 3 vols. 1913. (Must be used with care and checked against original records.)

——. *Genealogical and Family History of Western New York.* 3 vols. 1912. (Must be used with care and checked against original records.)

Daughters of the American Revolution, New York, Manhattan Chapter. *Old Homesteads and Historic Buildings, Genealogy and Family Lore.* 1930.

Documentary History of the State of New York. Edited by E. B. O'Callaghan. 4 vols. 1849–51. (Valuable, but not indexed.)

Documents Relative to the Colonial History of the State of New York. 15 vols. 1853–87.

Evjen, John Oluf. *Scandinavian Immigrants in New York, 1630–74.* 1916.

Fernow, Berthold. *Calendar of Wills on File and Recorded in the Offices of the Clerk of the Court of Appeals, of the County Clerk at Albany, and of the Secretary of State, 1626–1836.* 1896.

——. *New Amsterdam Family Names and Their Origin.* 1898.

Flagg, Charles Allcott. *Bibliography of New York Colonial History.* 1901. (New York State Library, Bulletin 56.)

MacWethy, Lou D. *The Book of Names Especially Relating to the Early Palatines and the First Settlers in the Mohawk Valley.* 1933.

New York (Colony). *Calendar of New York Colonial Commissions, 1680–1770.* 1929.

——. *Colonial Records. General Entries, Vol. I, 1664–65.* 1899.

——. *Names of Persons for Whom Marriage Licenses Were Issued by the Secretary of the Province of New York, Previous to 1784.* (A supplement was issued in New York State Library, Bulletin: History, No. 1.)

——. *New York Marriage Licenses.* 1916(?). (Another supplement to the above, originally issued in *New York Genealogical and Biographical Record,* beginning July 1915.)

New York (City) Orphan Masters. *The Minutes of the Orphanmasters of New Amsterdam, 1655 to 1663.* 2 vols. 1902–7.

New York (County) Surrogate's Court. *Abstracts of Wills on File in the Surrogate's Office, City of New York.* 1893–1913. (New York Historical Society, *Collections.*)

New York (State) State Historian. *Ecclesiastical Records, State of New York.* 7 vols. 1901–16.

———. *Handbook of Historical and Patriotic Societies in New York State, Including List of Local Historians.* 1926.

New York Genealogical and Biographical Society. *Collections.* 1890–.

New York Historical Society. *Collections.* 11 vols. 1811–59.

———. *Collections.* 1868–. (Another series.)

Pelletreau, William Smith. *Early Long Island Wills of Suffolk County, 1691–1703.* 1897.

———. *Early Wills of Westchester County, New York, from 1664 to 1784.* 1898.

———. *Historic Homes and Institutions and Genealogical and Family History of New York.* 4 vols. 1907. (Should be used with care.)

Reynolds, Cuyler. *Genealogical and Family History of Southern New York and the Hudson River Valley.* 3 vols. 1914. (Must be used with care.)

———. *Hudson-Mohawk Genealogical and Family Memoirs.* 4 vols. 1911. (Must be used with care.)

Robison, Mrs. Jeannie Floyd (Jones). *Genealogical Records: Manuscript Entries of Births, Deaths and Marriages, Taken from Family Bibles, 1581–1917.* 1917.

Seversmith, Herbert Furman. *Long Island Genealogical Source Material.* Washington, 1949. (This is another "special publication" of the National Genealogical Society.)

Stillwell, John Edwin. *Historical and Genealogical Miscellany: Data Relating to the Settlement and Settlers of New York and New Jersey.* 4 vols. 1903–15.

Talcott, Sebastian Visscher. *Genealogical Notes of New York and New England Families.* 1883.

Toler, Henry Pennington. *The New Harlem Register.* 1903.

Turner, Orsamus. *History of the Pioneer Settlement of Phelps and Gorham's Purchase, and Morris' Reserve.* 1852.

———. *Pioneer History of the Holland Purchase of Western New York.* 1850.

United States Bureau of the Census. *Heads of Families at the First Census of the United States Taken in the Year 1790: New York.* 1908.

Your Ancestors: A National Magazine of Genealogy and Family

History. Buffalo, N.Y., 1947–. (This mimeographed monthly grew out of a newspaper column; in a sense it takes the place of *Early Settlers of New York State,* which ceased publication in 1942.)

12. NORTH CAROLINA

Arthur, John Preston. *Western North Carolina; a History (from 1730 to 1913).* 1914.

Clemens, William Montgomery. *North and South Carolina Marriage Records. ca.* 1927.

Draughton, Wallace R. *North Carolina Genealogical Reference: A Research Guide.* Durham, 1956. (A guide to "state archives, church, and county court" records; included is a list of genealogists and those who want to exchange records.)

Fries, Adelaide Lisetta, ed. *Records of the Moravians in North Carolina.* 7 vols. Raleigh, 1922–47. (This important set of records, published by the North Carolina Historical Commission, covers 1752 to 1822. Miss Fries wrote several historical accounts of the Moravians in the Carolinas and Georgia, which should be consulted.)

Hunter, C. L. *Sketches of Western North Carolina, Historical and Biographical.* 1877.

North Carolina (Colony). *The Colonial Records of North Carolina.* 10 vols. 1886–90.

North Carolina (State) Secretary of State. *Abstract of North Carolina Wills.* 1910.

———. *North Carolina Wills and Inventories.* 1912.

North Carolina Historical and Genealogical Register. 3 vols. 1900–3.

United States Bureau of the Census. *Heads of Families at the First Census of the United States Taken in the Year 1790: North Carolina.* 1908.

Wheeler, John Hill. *Historical Sketches of North Carolina from 1584 to 1851.* 1851. (It was reprinted in 1925.)

Whitener, Daniel Jay. *Local History—How to Find It and Write It.* Asheville, 1955. (Contains a bibliography of North Carolina county histories.)

13. PENNSYLVANIA

Browning, Charles Henry. *Welsh Settlement of Pennsylvania.* 1912.

Colonial Records of Pennsylvania. 16 vols. 1851–53. (Continued as *Pennsylvania Archives.*)

Egle, William Henry. *Pennsylvania Genealogies: Scotch-Irish and German.* 1886.

———. *Some Pennsylvania Women during the War of the Revolution.* 1898.

Genealogical Society of Pennsylvania. *Publications.* 1895–.

Historical Journal: A Quarterly Record of Local History and Gene-

alogy, Devoted Principally to Northwestern Pennsylvania. 2 vols. 1888–94.

Historical Record of Wyoming Valley. 14 vols. 1887–1908.

Historical Register: Notes and Queries, Historical and Genealogical, Relating to Interior Pennsylvania. 2 vols. 1883–84.

Hoenstine, Floyd G. *Guide to Genealogical and Historical Research in Pennsylvania.* Holidaysburg, Pa., 1958. (This is a mimeographed index to "all known publications containing information on families residing in the famous Juniata Valley . . . the Susquehanna Valley and all of central Pennsylvania.")

Jordan, John Woolf. *Genealogical and Personal History of Northern Pennsylvania.* 3 vols. 1913. (Must be used with care.)

——. *Genealogical and Personal History of the Allegheny Valley.* 3 vols. 1913. (Must be used with care.)

——. *Genealogical and Personal History of Western Pennsylvania.* 3 vols. 1915. (Must be used with care.)

——. *Historic Homes and Institutions and Genealogical Memoirs of the Lehigh Valley.* 2 vols. 1905. (Must be used with care.)

Keith, Charles Penrose. *Chronicles of Pennsylvania from the English Revolution to the Peace of Aix-la-Chapelle, 1688–1748.* 2 vols. 1917.

——. *The Provincial Councillors of Pennsylvania Who Held Office between 1733 and 1776.* 1883.

Kittochtinny Historical Society. *Papers.* 1900–.

Kittochtinny Magazine: A Tentative Record of Local History and Genealogy West of the Susquehanna. 1905. (Only one volume was published.)

Lancaster County Historical Society. *Historical Papers and Addresses.* 1897–.

Meginness, John Franklin. *Biographical Annals of Deceased Residents of the West Branch Valley of the Susquehanna.* 1889.

——. *Otzinachson: A History of the West Branch Valley of the Susquehanna.* 1857. (Reprinted in 1889.)

Myers, Albert Cook. *Immigration of the Irish Quakers into Pennsylvania, 1682–1750.* 1902.

——. *Quaker Arrivals at Philadelphia, 1682–1750.* 1902.

Northampton County Historical and Genealogical Society. *Publications.* 1926–.

Penn Germania. 1900–.

Pennsylvania Archives. 1852–.

Pennsylvania Genealogical Magazine. 1948–. The first 15 volumes of this were called Publications of the Genealogical Society of Pennsylvania.)

Pennsylvania-German. 12 vols. 1900–11.

Pennsylvania German Society. *Proceedings and Addresses.* 1891–.

Pennsylvania Magazine of History and Biography. 1877–. (In 1954, a consolidated index to Vols. 1–75, 1877–1951, was published.

Not all personal names are indexed; however, under the heading "Genealogical Material Incompletely Indexed" are hundreds of references to "family histories and notes" in alphabetical order by surname; look also under the heading "Lists, Unindexed or Partially Indexed," for there are given references to many documents which contain lists of personal names, signatures, for example.)

Rupp, Israel Daniel. *A Collection of Upwards of Thirty Thousand Names of German, Swiss, Dutch, French and Other Immigrants in Pennsylvania from 1727 to 1776.* 1931. (Earlier editions in 1856 and 1876.)

Strassburger, Ralph Beaver. *Pennsylvania German Pioneers; a Publication of the Original Lists of Arrivals in the Port of Philadelphia from 1727 to 1808.* 3 vols. 1934. (Pennsylvania German Society, *Proceedings*, Vols. 42–44.)

United States Bureau of the Census. *Heads of Families at the First Census of the United States Taken in the Year 1790: Pennsylvania.* 1908.

Western Pennsylvania Historical Magazine. 1918–.

Wyoming Historical and Geological Society. *Proceedings and Collections.* 1858–.

Your Family Tree. Indiana, Pa., 1948–. (This is a mimeographed periodical. It includes abstracts of many original records in western Pennsylvania.)

14. RHODE ISLAND

Arnold, James Newell. *The Records of the Proprietors of the Narragansett, Otherwise Called the Fones Records.* 1894.

————. *Vital Record of Rhode Island, 1636–1850.* 21 vols. 1891. (Contains transcripts of the vital records of the several towns, indexes to obituary notices, and so forth.)

Austin, John Osborne. *The Genealogical Dictionary of Rhode Island, Comprising Three Generations of Settlers Who Came before 1690.* 1887. (Austin's *Dictionary.*)

Chapin, Howard Miller. *Documentary History of Rhode Island.* 2 vols. 1916–19. (Verbatim reprints of the earliest, seventeenth-century documents, including the signatories.)

————. *Rhode Island in the Colonial Wars. A List of Rhode Island Soldiers and Sailors in King George's War, 1740–48.* 1920.

————. *Rhode Island in the Colonial Wars. A List of Rhode Island Soldiers and Sailors in the Old French and Indian War, 1755–62.* 1918.

————. *Rhode Island Privateers in King George's War, 1739–48.* 1926.

Hopkins, Charles Wyman. *The Home Lots of the Early Settlers of the Providence Plantations.* 1886.

Narragansett Historical Register. 9 vols. 1882–91.

Newport Historical Magazine, see the *Rhode Island Historical Magazine.*

Newport Historical Society. *Bulletin.* 1912–.

Representative Men and Old Families of Rhode Island. 3 vols. 1908. (Use with care.)

Rhode Island (Colony) Court of Trials. *Rhode Island Court Records: Records of the Court of Trials of the Colony of Providence Plantations, 1647–70.* 2 vols. 1920–22.

Rhode Island (Colony) General Assembly. *Census of the Inhabitants of the Colony of Rhode Island and Providence Plantations, Taken . . . in the Year 1774.* 1858.

―――. *Records of the Colony (and of the State) of Rhode Island, and Providence Plantations.* 10 vols. 1856–65. (Covers 1636–1792.)

Rhode Island Historical Magazine. 7 vols. 1880–87. (The first four volumes were called the *Newport Historical Magazine.*)

Rhode Island Historical Society. *Collections.* 1827–.

―――. *Proceedings.* 34 vols. 1872–1914.

―――. *Publications.* 8 vols. 1893–1900.

Rhode Island Historical Tracts. 1877–.

Rhode Island Land Evidences, Vol. I, 1648–96. Abstracts, 1921. (All that was published; the four volumes of the original documents are in the State Archives, State House, Providence, R.I., 02902.)

Smith, Joseph Jencks. *Civil and Military List of Rhode Island, 1647–1800.* 1900.

―――. *Civil and Military List of Rhode Island, 1800–50.* 1901.

―――. *New Index to the Civil and Military Lists of Rhode Island.* 1907.

United States Bureau of the Census. *Heads of Families at the First Census of the United States Taken in the Year 1790: Rhode Island.* 1908.

15. SOUTH CAROLINA

Clemens, William Montgomery. *North and South Carolina Marriage Records, from the Earliest Days to the Civil War. ca.* 1927.

Davis, Harry Alexander. *Some Huguenot Families of South Carolina and Georgia.* 1927.

Salley, Alexander Samuel. *Death Notices in the South Carolina Gazette, 1732–75.* 1917.

―――. *Marriage Notices in the South Carolina and American General Gazette from May 30, 1766, to February 28, 1781, and in Its Successor, the Royal Gazette (1781–82).* 1914.

―――. *Marriage Notices in the South Carolina Gazette; and Country Journal (1765–75) and in the Charlestown Gazette (1778–80).* 1904.

————. *Marriage Notices in the South Carolina Gazette and Its Successors (1732–1801).* 1902.

South Carolina Historical Commission. *Bulletins.* 1915–.

————. *Warrants for Lands in South Carolina, 1672–79.* 1910.

South Carolina Historical and Genealogical Magazine. 1900–.

South Carolina Historical Society. *Collections.* 1857–.

————. *Proceedings.* 1931–.

United States Bureau of the Census. *Heads of Families at the First Census of the United States Taken in the Year 1790: South Carolina.* 1908.

16. VERMONT

Biographical Encyclopaedia of Vermont of the Nineteenth Century. Edited by Henry Clay Williams. 1885.

Carleton, Hiram. *Genealogical and Family History of the State of Vermont.* 2 vols. 1903. (Use with care and check against original records.)

Clark, Byron N. *A List of Pensioners of the War of 1812.* 1904.

Comstock, John M. *The Congregational Churches of Vermont and Their Ministers, 1762–1914.* 1915.

Crocker, Henry. *History of the Baptists in Vermont.* 1913.

DeGoesbriand, Louis. *Catholic Memoirs of Vermont and New Hampshire.* 1886.

Dodge, Prentiss Cutler. *Encyclopedia, Vermont Biography.* 1912.

Gilman, Marcus Davis. *The Bibliography of Vermont.* 1897.

Hemenway, Abby Maria. *The Vermont Historical Gazetteer.* 5 vols. 1868–91. (A complete index was published in 1923.)

Hills, Frederick Simon. *Men of Vermont State.* 1925–.

Jeffrey, William Hartley. *Successful Vermonters: A Modern Gazetteer of Lamoille, Franklin and Grand Isle Counties.* 1907.

Protestant Episcopal Church in the United States of America, Vermont Diocese. *Documentary History of the Protestant Episcopal Church in the Diocese of Vermont.* 1870.

Ullery, Jacob G. *Men of Vermont: An Illustrated Biographical History.* 1894.

United States Bureau of the Census. *Heads of Families at the First Census of the United States Taken in the Year 1790: Vermont.* 1907.

Vermont. *Records of the Governor and Council of the State of Vermont.* 8 vols. 1873–80. (Covers the years 1775 to 1836.)

Vermont, Secretary of State. *A List of the Principal Civil Officers of Vermont from 1777 to 1918.* 1918. (Earlier editions were known as *Deming's Vermont Officers.*)

Vermont Antiquarian. 3 vols. 1902–5.

Vermont Historical Society. *Collections.* 2 vols. 1870–71.

————. *Proceedings.* 1860–.

Vermont Marriages, 1903. (Unfortunately only one volume was issued.)

Vermont Year-book. 1818–. (Formerly called *Walton's Vermont Register.* Valuable for brief information regarding the history of each town.)

17. VIRGINIA

Boogher, William Fletcher. *Gleanings of Virginia History: An Historical and Genealogical Collection, Largely from Original Sources.* 1903.

Brock, Robert Alonzo. *Documents, Chiefly Unpublished, Relating to the Huguenot Emigration to Virginia.* 1886.

————. *Virginia and Virginians.* 2 vols. 1888.

Casey, Joseph J. *Personal Names in Hening's Statutes at Large of Virginia, and Shepherd's Continuation.* 1933. (An earlier edition was published in 1896.)

Clemens, William Montgomery. *Virginia Wills before 1799.* 1924.

Crozier, William Armstrong. *Early Virginia Marriages.* 1907.

————. *A Key to Southern Pedigrees.* 1911.

————. *Virginia Colonial Militia, 1651–1776.* 1905.

————. *Virginia Heraldica, Being a Registry of Virginia Gentry Entitled to Coat Armor, with Genealogical Notes of the Families.* 1908.

————. *Westmoreland County.* 1913. (Contains abstracts of Westmoreland County wills, 1655–1794.)

————. *Williamsburg Wills.* 1906.

Fothergill, Mrs. Augusta Bridgland (Middleton). *Wills of Westmoreland County, Virginia, 1654–1800.* 1925.

Jester, Annie Lash, ed. *Adventures of Purse and Person.* Princeton, 1956. (The first "muster roll" of the Virginia Colony, 1624/ 25, is printed in full in this important book; it is followed by a genealogical account of 109 of those who "adventured" and their descendants through the third generation.)

Johnston, David Emmons. *A History of Middle New River Settlements and Contiguous Territory.* 1906.

Johnston, Frederick. *Memorials of Old Virginia Clerks, Arranged Alphabetically by Counties with Complete Index of Names, and Dates of Service from 1634 to the Present Time.* 1888.

Long, Charles Massie. *Virginia County Names: Two Hundred and Seventy Years of Virginia History.* 1908.

McWhorter, Lucullus Virgil. *The Border Settlers of Northwestern Virginia from 1768 to 1795.* 1915.

Meade, William. *Old Churches, Ministers and Families of Virginia.* 2 vols. 1897. (Earlier editions were published in 1857, 1861, and 1878; indexes were published by J. M. Toner in 1898, and J. C. Wise in 1910. This is known as Bishop Meade's *Old Churches.*)

Researcher: A Magazine of History and Genealogical Exchange. 2 vols. 1926–28.

Swem, Earl Gregg. *Virginia Historical Index.* 2 vols. 1934–35.

(Indexes the personal names and subjects in seven important Virginia magazines and collections.)

Stanard, William Glover. *The Colonial Virginia Register: A List of Governors, Councillors and Other Higher Officials, and Also of Members of the House of Burgesses, and the Revolutionary Conventions of the Colony of Virginia.* 1902.

——. *Some Emigrants to Virginia.* 2d ed., enlarged. 1915. (Earlier edition in 1911.)

Stewart, Robert Armistead. *Index to Printed Virginia Genealogies.* 1930. (A bibliography, not an index of personal names.)

Torrence, Clayton. *Virginia Wills and Administrations, 1632–1800: An Index of Wills Recorded in Local Courts of Virginia, 1632– 1800.* 1931. (Includes also inventories and administrations of estates of intestates.)

Tyler's Quarterly Historical and Genealogical Magazine. 1919–.

United States Bureau of the Census. *Heads of Families at the First Census of the United States Taken in the Year 1790: Virginia.* 1908. ("The federal census schedules of the state of Virginia for 1790 are missing, the lists of the state enumerations made in 1782, 1783, 1784, and 1785, while not complete, have been substituted.")

Valentine, Edward Pleasants. *The Edward Pleasants Valentine Papers.* 4 vols. 1927.

Van Meter, Benjamin Franklin. *Genealogies and Sketches of Some Old Families Who Have Taken Prominent Part in the Development of Virginia and Kentucky Especially.* 1901.

The Virginia Genealogist, 1957–. Washington. (This is one of the newest of the genealogical journals; it deals with Virginia records.)

Virginia Historical Society. *Collections.* 12 vols. 1833–92.

Virginia Magazine of History and Biography. 1893–.

Virginia State Library. *Annual Report.* (Several of the annual reports of this library contain valuable bibliographies and lists.)

——. *Bulletin.* (Several of these bulletins contain valuable bibliographies and lists.)

Wayland, John Walter. *Virginia Valley Records.* 1930.

William and Mary College Quarterly Historical Magazine. 1892–.

Willison, George Findlay. *Behold Virginia, the Fifth Crown: Being the Trials, Adventures & Disasters of the First Families of Virginia, the Rise of the Grandees & the Eventual Triumph of the Common & Uncommon Sort in the Revolution.* New York, 1951. (A narrative account of the early history of Virginia well worth the genealogist's while.)

APPENDIX B

States Whose Offices of Vital Statistics Have Records Dating before 1900

For the convenience of ancestor hunters there are listed below the states which have collected in a state office the vital records from their several towns and counties.

In using this list, it should be remembered that in nearly all cases the records for the earlier years are scattered and incomplete. Not all states have made an effort, as Vermont has, to collect from the local governments the vital records which are on file. Therefore, failing information from the state office, the searcher should try the town or county in which his ancestors lived.

In many of the more recently established states the county clerk seems to be the repository for marriage records, and in some cases for birth and death records.

In Louisiana the political unit corresponding to the county is the parish; hence the clerk of the parish court is the individual with whom vital records are deposited.

In some states, notably Connecticut, New York, Pennsylvania, and Virginia, the state library has become the custodian of the old record books. In such states application for the information desired must be made to the state librarian.

Some states furnish free copies of vital records, but charge a fee for certified copies for legal use and use in establishing lineages for membership in patriotic societies; other states charge a fee for any kind of copy.

This list has been greatly condensed from an article in the *New England Historical and Genealogical Register*, Vol. 90 (January 1936). pp. 9–31. Harold Clarke Durrell, the compiler of this article, gave very full information about the activities of the offices in all the states, so his article should be consulted for full details.

Arizona. State Board of Health, Phoenix. Scattered birth records since 1855, and death records since 1878.
Connecticut. Bureau of Vital Statistics, Station A, Drawer K, Hart-

ford. Records since 1 July 1897. For older records try the State Library, Hartford.

Delaware. Bureau of Vital Statistics, State House, Dover. Births since 1861; marriages since 1847; deaths since 1881.

District of Columbia. Bureau of Vital Statistics, Health Department, Washington. Births since 1871, deaths since 1855. Marriages since 1811 at Supreme Court of the District of Columbia.

Florida. Bureau of Vital Statistics, State Board of Health, Jacksonville. Births since 1865, deaths since 1877. Marriage records are kept in county offices.

Iowa. Curator, Historical Building, State House, Des Moines. Births, marriages, and deaths since 1880.

Louisiana. State Registrar, Bureau of Vital Statistics, New Court House Building, New Orleans. Scattered births and deaths since 1819. Marriage records are kept in parish courthouses.

Maine. Department of Vital Statistics, Bureau of Health, Augusta. Births, marriages, and deaths since 1892, with scattered records before that date.

Maryland. Bureau of Vital Statistics, State Department of Health, 2411 N. Charles Street, Baltimore. Births and deaths since 1898.

Massachusetts. Bureau of Vital Statistics, Secretary of the Commonwealth, Boston. Births, marriages, and deaths since 1850, with incomplete records for 1841–49.

Michigan. Bureau of Records and Statistics, Department of Health, Lansing. Births and deaths since 1867 (incomplete). Try the state library for earlier records.

New Hampshire. Department of Vital Statistics, State House, Concord. Some records back to 1640, as town records have been copied and are on file.

New Jersey. Bureau of Vital Statistics, State Department of Health, State House, Trenton. Births, marriages, and deaths since 1848. County clerks have marriage records in some cases back to colonial times.

New York. State Department of Health, Albany. Births, marriages, and deaths since 1895. Try the State Library for older records, especially state census records.

Rhode Island. State Registrar of Vital Statistics, Room 353, State Office Building, Providence. Births, marriages, and deaths since 1853.

Vermont. Secretary of State, Montpelier. All births, marriages, and deaths from the earliest times, as recorded in town records, have been copied and sent to this office. Also cemetery inscriptions from many towns.

Virginia. Bureau of Vital Statistics, State Department of Health, Richmond. Births, marriages, and deaths since 1853.

Wisconsin. Bureau of Vital Statistics, State Board of Health, Madison. Births and deaths since 1852, marriages since 1840 (although scattered for early years).

Supplementary Note

Several of the handbooks, listed in section A, Appendix A, tell you where to write for vital records, but the three pamphlets listed below covering all states and territories, compiled by the National Office of Vital Statistics, Public Health Service, United States Department of Health, Education, and Welfare, are available from the Superintendent of Documents, United States Government Printing Office, Washington, D.C. 20402, at the prices indicated. In ordering, remember that postage stamps are not accepted in payment, so you must either risk sending coins through the mails or get a postal money order.

Where to Write for Birth and Death Records. 1967. (Public Health Service Publication No. 630A, 15¢.)

Where to Write for Marriage Records. 1965. (Public Health Service Publication No. 630B, 10¢.)

Where to Write for Divorce Records. 1965. (Public Health Service Publication No. 630C, 10¢.)

APPENDIX C

Census Records

The National Archives and Records Service, General Services Administration, Washington, D.C. 20408, has published on a single sheet a brief description of each census and will supply an order form (GSA Form 7029) for copies of specific records. (See the further comment on pages 106–115.)

The records of the later censuses are practically complete, and in many cases duplicate copies of the census of 1850 and those following are to be found in the state historical societies, state libraries, or other state offices.

In many states a census has been taken halfway between the federal censuses. Thus, in New York there was a census in 1855; another in 1865, and so forth. The ancestor hunter should dig around and try to find out what censuses have been taken in the locality in which he is interested.

Population Schedules Missing, 1790 to 1820

This list of missing schedules is reprinted from Mrs. Spencer's list for two reasons: to save the ancestor hunter time and postage in writing to Washington, and in the hope that by lucky chance some reader of this book may find one or more of these schedules and notify the Bureau of the Census of the find in order that copies may be made.

CENSUS RECORDS OF 1800, 1810, AND 1820, ON FILE
IN WASHINGTON
(Figures Indicate Number of Volumes)

State Schedules	1800	1810	1820
Connecticut	2	3	3
Delaware	1	1	1
District of Columbia (in Maryland)	1	....	1
Georgia	....	....	5
Illinois	....	....	2
Indiana	....	....	3
Kentucky	....	4	8

State Schedules	1800	1810	1820
Louisiana	....	1	2
Maine	3	2	4
Maryland	3	4	7
Massachusetts	4	5	8
Michigan	....	....	1
Mississippi	....	....	1
New Hampshire	1	2	2
New Jersey			
New York	8	9	18
North Carolina	5	6	6
Ohio	....	....	11
Pennsylvania	7	11	18
Rhode Island	1	1	1
South Carolina	2	2	3
Tennessee	....	(1 county)	3
Vermont	2	2	3
Virginia	....	6	11

1790 SCHEDULES MISSING

Delaware (all).
Georgia (all).
Kentucky (all).
Maryland (Alleghany, Calvert, and Somerset counties).
New Jersey (all).
North Carolina (Caswell, Granville, and Orange counties).
Tennessee (all).
Virginia (all—the printed volume of schedules is made up of state tax lists, not census).

1800 SCHEDULES MISSING

Georgia (all).
Indiana Territory (all).
Kentucky (all).
Maine (part of York County).
Maryland (Baltimore County outside of the city of Baltimore).
Massachusetts (part of Suffolk County).
Mississippi Territory (all).
New Hampshire (parts of Rockingham and Strafford counties).
New Jersey (all).
Northwest Territory Ohio River (all).
Pennsylvania (parts of Westmoreland County).
South Carolina (Richland County).
Tennessee (all).
Virginia (all).

1810 SCHEDULES MISSING

District of Columbia (all).
Georgia (all).
Illinois Territory (all except Randolph County).
Indiana Territory (all).
Louisiana (all).
Maine (part of Oxford County).
Michigan (all).
Mississippi (all).
New Jersey (all).
New York (Cortland and part of Broome counties).
North Carolina (Craven, Green, New Hanover, and Wake counties).
Ohio (all).
Pennsylvania (parts of Bedford, Philadelphia, and Cumberland counties).
Tennessee (all except Rutherford County).
Virginia (Cabell, Grayson, Greenbrier, Halifax, Hardy, Henry, James, King William, Lee, Louisa, Mecklenburg, Nansemond, Northampton, Orange, Patrick, Pittsylvania, Russell, and Tazewell counties).

1820 SCHEDULES MISSING

Alabama (all).
Arkansas Territory (all).
Georgia (Franklin, Rabun, and Twiggs counties).
Indiana (Daviess County).
Maine (parts of Penobscot and Washington counties).
Missouri (all).
New Hampshire (Grafton and parts of Rockingham and Strafford counties).
New Jersey (all).
North Carolina (Currituck, Franklin, Montgomery, Randolph, and Wake counties).
Ohio (Franklin and Wood counties).
Pennsylvania (parts of Lancaster and Luzerne counties).
Tennessee (Anderson, Bledsoe, Blount, Campbell, Carter, Claiborne, Cocke, Grainger, Greene, Hawkins, Hamilton, Jefferson, Knox, McMinn, Marion, Monroe, Morgan, Rhea, Roane, Sevier, Sullivan, and Washington counties).

Supplementary Note

Since 1937 the following substitutes for the missing census schedules of 1790 have been compiled from tax lists, similar to those constituting the Virginia volume cited in Appendix A.

Delaware: *Reconstructed 1790 Census of Delaware.* Compiled by Leon DeValinger. Washington, 1954. (National Genealogical Society, Special Publication No. 10.)

Kentucky: *"First Census" of Kentucky, 1790.* Compiled by Charles
B. Heinemann and Gaius Marcus Brumbaugh. Washington [*ca.*
1940].
Kentucky: *"Second Census" of Kentucky, 1800.* Compiled by G.
Glenn Clift. Frankfort, Ky., 1954.
Vermont: *Heads of Families at the Second Census of the United
States Taken in the year 1800: Vermont.* Montpelier, Vt., 1938.

All the extant schedules of the federal census 1800–80 have
been reproduced on microfilm. The reels containing the records of
the area in which you are interested may be purchased separately,
if you do not find them in the genealogical library which you use.
You can get price lists from the National Archives and Records
Service. These are the titles of the price lists:

United States National Archives. *Special List No. 8: Population
Schedules, 1800–1870, Volume Index to Counties and Major
Cities.* 1951 (reissued 1957).
United States National Archives. *Federal Population Censuses,
1840–1880, a Price List of Microfilm Copies of the Original
Schedules.* 1957.
United States National Archives. *List of National Archives Micro-
film Publications, 1953.* 1953. (Under the designation RG, pp.
74–79, the census schedules for 1800–30 are listed by states and
counties, with the prices for each unit.)

Additional Supplementary Note to Fourth Edition

Since 1960 many new publications have appeared dealing with
census records, too many to digest in this introduction to genealogical research. The improvement of microfilming has made possible the reproduction of many census records, and the development of branches of the National Archives, known as Federal
Records Centers, in ten or a dozen urban areas where microfilms
of many groups of records in the National Archives, including the
census records, may be read, or from which they may be borrowed
under specified terms by libraries throughout the country, has
made it much easier for genealogists, professional and amateur, to
gain access to them. Special List No. 34 from the National Archives and Records Service, entitled *Federal Population and Mor-
tality Census Schedules, 1790–1890, in the National Archives and
the States,* compiled by W. Neil Franklin (1971), tells you not
only what census records are available but what libraries and institutions have copies of them, either in manuscript or on microfilm.

As something of a guide to the sources which exist I have let
this appendix stand as it was printed in the third edition of this
book, merely adding this note, mainly because it seems impossible
to digest and condense into the space available the eighty-nine
pages of the compilation by Mr. Franklin.

A Bibliography of Lists, Registers, Rolls, and Rosters of Revolutionary War Soldiers

This bibliography is not exhaustive, and no attempt has been made to include every list of Revolutionary soldiers which may have been published. It does, however, contain the most important official and semiofficial lists published for the thirteen original states and Vermont, Maine, and Kentucky.

For convenience in use, the lists are arranged by states. Several general lists have been added at the end as they cover soldiers from several states. In addition there have been included in this general classification the more useful lists of soldiers who are buried in states which have come into existence since 1783.

A copy of every book listed will be found in the Library of Congress in Washington, and undoubtedly the majority of the volumes may be found in other genealogical collections.

Connecticut

Connecticut Adjutant-General's Office. *Record of Service of Connecticut Men in I. War of the Revolution.* Hartford, 1889.

Connecticut Historical Society. *Lists and Returns of Connecticut Men in the Revolution, 1775–83.* Hartford, 1909. (*Collections of the Connecticut Historical Society,* Vol. 12.)

————. *Rolls and Lists of Connecticut Men in the Revolution, 1775–83.* Hartford, 1901. (*Collections of the Connecticut Historical Society,* Vol. 8.)

Note: The three above-mentioned volumes supplement one another.

United States Pension Bureau. *Pension Records of the Revolutionary Soldiers from Connecticut.* Washington, 1919. (In Daughters of the American Revolution, *Twenty-First Report, 1917–18,* pp. 131–299.)

Delaware

Bellas, Henry Hobart. *A History of the Delaware Society of the*

Cincinnati. Wilmington, 1895. (*Papers of the Historical Society of Delaware,* No. 13.)

Delaware Public Archives Commission. *Delaware Archives.* Wilmington, 1911–. (Contains many regimental histories and rolls and rosters.)

Whiteley, William Gustavus. *The Revolutionary Soldiers of Delaware.* Wilmington, 1896. (*Papers of the Historical Society of Delaware,* No. 14.)

Georgia

Georgia Department of Archives and History. *Georgia's Roster of the Revolution.* Atlanta, 1920.

―――. *Revolutionary Soldiers' Receipts for Georgia Bounty Grants.* Atlanta, 1928.

Houston, Martha Lou. *600 Revolutionary Soldiers Living in Georgia in 1827–8.* Washington, 1932.

Kentucky

Quisenberry, Anderson Chenault, compiler. *Revolutionary Soldiers in Kentucky.* Louisville, 1896. (In Sons of the American Revolution, Kentucky Society, *Yearbook,* pp. 49–278.)

Maine

Flagg, Charles Allcott. *An Alphabetical Index of Revolutionary Pensioners Living in Maine.* Dover, 1920. (Reprinted from *Sprague's Journal of Maine History.*)

House, Charles J. *Names of Soldiers of the American Revolution Who Applied for State Bounty.* Augusta, 1893.

Note: It should be remembered that Maine was a part of Massachusetts at the time of the Revolution, and therefore the Massachusetts rolls should be consulted.

Maryland

Maryland Historical Society. *Muster Rolls and Other Records of Service of Maryland Troops in the American Revolution, 1775–83.* Baltimore, 1900. (*Archives of Maryland,* Vol. 18.)

Newman, Harry Wright. *Maryland Revolutionary Records.* 1938.

Massachusetts

Draper, Mrs. Belle (Merrill). *Honor Roll of Massachusetts Patriots Heretofore Unknown, Being a List of Men and Women Who Loaned Money to the Federal Government during the Years 1777–79.* Boston, 1899.

Note: According to the preface of this book, descendants of these men and women are eligible for membership in the D.A.R.; hence this title is included in this bibliography.

Massachusetts Secretary of the Commonwealth. *Massachusetts Sol-*

diers and Sailors of the Revolutionary War. 17 vols. Boston, 1896–1908.

New Hampshire

Hammond, Isaac Weare. *Rolls of the Soldiers of the Revolutionary War.* 4 vols. Concord, 1885–89. (*New Hampshire: Provincial and State Papers,* Vols. 14–17.)

New Jersey

New Jersey Adjutant-General's Office. *Official Register of the Officers and Men of New Jersey in the Revolutionary War.* Trenton, 1872.

New York

New York (State) Comptroller's Office. *New York in the Revolution as Colony and State.* 2 vols. Albany, 1901–4.
————. *New York in the Revolution as Colony and State.* Albany, 1898.
New York (State) Secretary of State. *The Balloting Book, and Other Documents Relating to Military Bounty Lands, in the State of New York.* Albany, 1825.
New York (State) University. *New York in the Revolution.* Albany, 1887. (*Documents Relating to the Colonial History of the State of New York,* Vol. 15.)

North Carolina

Blair, Anna. *A List of Revolutionary Soldiers Buried in North Carolina.* 1926. (In *Historical Collections of the Georgia Chapters, Daughters of the American Revolution,* Vol. 1, pp. 352–64.)
Daughters of the American Revolution, North Carolina. *Roster of the Soldiers from North Carolina in the American Revolution.* Durham, 1932.
North Carolina. *Roster of the Continental Line from North Carolina.* 1783. (In *The State Records of North Carolina,* Vol. 16, pp. 1002–1197. Consult also the index to this set, Vol. 4.)

Pennsylvania

Pennsylvania Archives. 2d series, Vols. 1, 3, 11, 13–15; 3d series, Vol. 23; 5th series, Vols. 1–8; 6th series, Vols. 1–2, 15.
Westcott, Thompson. *Names of Persons Who Took the Oath of Allegiance to the State of Pennsylvania, between the Years 1777 and 1789, with a History of the "Test Laws."* Philadelphia, 1865. (The descendants of those who took the oath are eligible for membership in the D.A.R.)

Rhode Island

Cowell, Benjamin. *Spirit of '76 in Rhode Island*. Boston, 1850. (An index to this volume may be found in James N. Arnold's *Vital Record of Rhode Island*, Vol. 12, pp. 91–298.)

Smith, Joseph Jencks. *Civil and Military List of Rhode Island, 1647–1850*. 3 vols. 1900–7. (Contains lists of the Revolutionary period.)

South Carolina

South Carolina Treasury. *Stub Entries of Indents Issued in Payment of Claims against South Carolina Growing Out of the Revolution*. Columbia, 1910.

Vermont

Crockett, Walter Hill. *Revolutionary Soldiers Interred in Vermont*. (In Vermont Historical Society, *Proceedings*, 1903–4, pp. 114–65; 1905–6, pp. 189–203.)

The Green Mountain Boys, and Men with Ethan Allen at Ticonderoga. (In the *Vermont Antiquarian*, Vol. 3, March 1905, pp. 138–43.)

Vermont. *Rolls of the Soldiers in the Revolutionary War, 1775 to 1783*. Rutland, 1904.

Virginia

Burgess, Louis Alexander. *Virginia Soldiers of 1776*. 2 vols. Richmond, 1927.

Stewart, Robert Armistead. "*Roster of the Virginia Navy of the Revolution*." In his *The History of Virginia's Navy of the Revolution*. 1934. Pp. 137–271.

Virginia State Library, Department of Archives and History. *List of the Revolutionary Soldiers of Virginia (with Supplement)*. Richmond, 1913. (Also published in its *Annual Report*, 1913.)

Miscellaneous General Lists

No attempt has been made to include in this category the several lists of Revolutionary soldiers buried in the various states, counties, and communities, which have been compiled by those interested in Revolutionary affairs. Genealogical libraries located in the specific region will have them and refer the searcher to them. There have been included in this general classification the more important and inclusive lists which cover more than one of the states forming the original federation.

Alabama Department of Archives and History. *Revolutionary Soldiers in Alabama*. 1911.

Armstrong, Zella. *Twenty-Four Hundred Tennessee Pensioners: Revolution, War of 1812. 1937.*

Danbridge, Mrs. Danske (Bedinger). *American Prisoners of the Revolution.* 1911.

Daughters of the American Revolution. *DAR Patriot Index.* Washington, 1966. (A supplement was issued in 1971. See pp. 126–127.)

Daughters of the American Revolution, Indiana. *American Revolutionary Soldiers and Patriots Buried in Indiana.* Compiled by Mrs. R. C. O'Byrne. 1938.

Heitman, Francis Bernard. *Historical Register of Officers of the Continental Army during the War of the Revolution, April, 1775, to December, 1783.* New revised and enlarged edition. Washington, 1914.

New York Historical Society. *Muster and Pay Rolls of the War of the Revolution, 1775–83. 1916.* (Contains records of troops in most of the original colonies and Canada.)

Ohio Adjutant-General's Office: *The Official Roster of the Soldiers of the American Revolution Buried in the State of Ohio.* 1929.

Saffell, William Thomas Roberts. *Records of the Revolutionary War.* 1858.

Silliman, Sue Imogene. *Michigan Military Records.* 1920. (Includes a list of Revolutionary soldiers buried in Michigan, and a list of pensioners who lived there.)

United States Department of State. *A Census of Pensioners for Revolutionary or Military Service.* 1841. (Compiled from records obtained in the Census of 1840.)

United States Pay Department (War Department). *Pierce's Register.* "Register of the Certificates Issued by John Pierce, Esquire, Paymaster General and Commissioner of Army Accounts for the United States," to Officers and Soldiers of the Continental Army under Act of July 4, 1783. (A reprint of the original edition of 1786 was published in the *Seventeenth Report of the Daughters of the American Revolution, 1913/14,* Washington, 1915, pp. 149–712.)

Walker, Mrs. Harriett J. *Revolutionary Soldiers Buried in Illinois.* 1917.

Supplementary Note

Rider's *The American Genealogical-Biographical Index,* 1952–, includes all the names in the above lists of Revolutionary War soldiers and others as well. I call your attention, however, to five lists of pensioners in addition to that of 1841 which is noted above. It is possible that your man may be found listed in one of them, having been overlooked in compilations of the rolls of those who served. Unfortunately there is no index to them.

"An Act Authorizing and Directing the Secretary of War to Place Certain Persons, herein named, on the Pension List." 4th Congress, 1st Session, Dec. 1795. (In *The Laws of the United States*, Philadelphia, Vol. 3, 1796, pp. 262–72. The earliest pension list I have found, arranged by states. A short list of about twenty-five names is found in Vol. 4, pp. 62–63, in another act passed in 1797.)

United States Laws, Statutes, etc. *Resolutions, Laws and Ordinances, Relating to the Pay, Half Pay, Commutation of Half Pay, Bounty Lands, and Other Promises Made by Congress to the Officers and Soldiers of the Revolution . . .* Washington, 1838. (Mainly the "private acts" for the relief of individuals named in them. There is an index, but not all names are included in it.)

United States War Department. *Letter from the Secretary of War Communicating a Transcript of the Pension List of the United States . . .* Washington, 1813. (A reprint was published by the Minnesota Historical Society in 1894.)

———. *Letter from the Secretary of War Transmitting a Report of the Name, Rank and Line, of Every Person Placed on the Pension List, in Pursuance of the Act of 18th March, 1818.* Washington, 1820.

———. *Report from the Secretary of War, in Obedience to Resolutions of the Senate of the 5th and 30th of June 1834, and the 3d of March, 1835, in Relation to the Pension Establishment of the United States.* 3 vols. Washington, 1835. (The list for each state is paged separately, and booksellers sometimes offer them in that way. Vol. 1 contains the New England states; Vol. 2, the middle states; and Vol. 3, the southern states and the District of Columbia.)

For a brief historical outline of the various acts of Congress authorizing pensions, see Dr. Jean Stephenson's *Is That Lineage Right?* (Washington, 1958), pp. 40–44.

Additional Supplementary Note to Fourth Edition

An Index of Revolutionary War Pension Applications. Washington, 1966. (Published by the National Genealogical Society, 1921 Sunderland Place N.W., Washington, D.C. 20036. This *Index* gives the pension number, which makes it easy to apply for photocopies of the papers accompanying the application. To secure these, special forms are required, which may be obtained by writing to the National Archives and Records Service, General Services Administration, Washington, D.C. 20408, and asking for GSA Form 6751—Order for Photocopies concerning Veterans, which you will have to fill out and return with your check for the fee named in it.)

Index

The names of fictitious people and imaginary places mentioned in the text are not included in this index. Neither are authors, editors, and titles of books listed in the bibliographies in the appendixes. Titles of books mentioned in the text are listed, followed in parentheses by the name of author or editor. Names of places are not usually included.